Complete Guide to
Outfield Play

Cliff Petrak

To Gary,
Sincerest Baseball Wishes,
Cliff Petrak

Harding Press
Haworth, New Jersey 07641

Library of Congress Cataloging-in-Publication Data

Petrak, Cliff
   Complete guide to outfield play / Cliff Petrak.
     p. cm.
   ISBN 1-890450-02-2
   1. Baseball—Defense. 2. Fielding (Baseball) I. Title.
GV867.7.P48 1997
796.357'24—dc21   97–32430
                                  CIP

ISBN 1-890450-02-2

Printed in the United States of America

HARDING PRESS
P. O. Box 141
Haworth, NJ 07641

Books by and for the coaching profession

Dedication

To Johnny Dichtel, Bob Krol, Kaz Darzinskis, Steve Dikowski, and Eddie Stoehr, my contemporary sandlot outfield heroes, who were the first to convince me by their consistent play and countless defensive gems that there was more to being outstanding in the outfield than to just be out standing in the outfield.

To Mickey Mantle, Willie Mays, Roberto Clemente, and Minnie Minoso, whose defensive play in the outfield excited me every bit as much as their times at bat.

To Tom Uraski and all my other fellow baseball coaches at Brother Rice High School who, along with all my former and present Crusader ballplayers, have done so much to keep me filled with a zest for life and a zeal for baseball.

ACKNOWLEDGMENTS

To photographers and friends Nick Ramirez and Martin Ritchey for giving of their time, talents, and equipment for this project.

To John Moran for his demonstrations in the many photographs of the fine techniques that he used as an outfielder.

To Br. Greg O'Donnell, C.F.C., Br. Frank Verre, C.F.C., and Cindy Kelly for the bounteous giving of their patience, time, and expertise in the use of their state-of-the-art technological hardware.

To St. Xavier University for the generous use of their baseball facility for our photo sessions.

Contents

Introduction

Beyond the infield dirt of every baseball diamond lies an area that constitutes about 85 percent of the fair territory of the entire field. Yet, it is patrolled by only one-third of the defensive team. So, we must wonder just what kind of ballplayer it takes to successfully handle those outer reaches of the ballpark.

They certainly aren't the pitchers the coaches rave about as controlling about 75 percent of the game. Nor are they the catchers who serve by leading the defense, guiding the pitchers, and controlling the game from behind the plate. And, unlike the infielders, the outfielders don't have to concern themselves with any "hot corner" smashes, balls to be scooped out of the dirt, double-play pivots, base-stealing threats, bunt fielding, tag plays, rundowns, or pickoffs. They don't even have to worry about avoiding some runner's flying spikes or ending up on the short end of a collision at a base.

It almost seems, then, that outfielders should perhaps be asked to pay their way into the ballpark. Unfortunately, many ballplayers believe, or are led to believe, that their positions make up the "leftovers" after the important positions have been doled out. It's no wonder, then, that outfielders often think of themselves as little more than a collection of non-pitchers, non-catchers, and non-infielders whose main worth and responsibility revolve around their offensive skills.

From a defensive perspective, many outfielders suffer from some degree of inferiority complex and why not? Many coaches find little more for them to do in practice than chasing down some lazy fly balls. Certainly, catching fly balls is an important skill. However, there is so much more to this position than most players and coaches take the time to investigate and drill.

Certainly, the outfielder's many duties and requisite talents have often been underestimated, but pitchers will tell you how appreciative they are to have three good ones around. On a long drive, the difference between a great catch and the ball falling in can change the entire outcome of a game. While the average number of game chances for an outfielder may be slightly less than for an infielder, outfield errors usually prove far more costly. Other than any adjacent outfielders, no one can help back up an outfielder except the fence.

Keeping drives from falling in and baserunners from taking an extra base on a hit is best remedied before the ball is hit...by more thoughtful, strategic positioning. While the lazy outfielder will allow himself to daydream of his next at bat, the involved outfielder will be constantly working his mind like a computer. He will be continuously weighing and analyzing numerous factors to place himself in the most strategic position possible. That's why the great outfielders seem to make so many more routine catches than the less experienced outfielders who fail to think out their most strategic positioning.

Remember, too, that not every outfield play will be a fly ball. Oftentimes, the play will involve the fielding of a hit...sometimes an extra-base hit. The approach, pickup, and throw must include the ingredients of efficiency, quickness, strength, and accuracy. Furthermore, whenever any hit is fielded with one or more runners on base, an almost instantaneous decision must be made. In what direction will the throw be made and why?

This decision to stop the lead runner or to instead concentrate on a backrunner is crucial strategy and also presents itself whenever a fly ball is caught with less than two outs and one or more runners on base. When outfielders find themselves thinking through these possible options before the ball is even hit to them, they know that they have really come of age as involved and "into-the-game" players.

The final several pages of each chapter contain descriptions of numerous drills to help ingrain the techniques and strategies discussed. After all, it is one thing to read about them, but quite another to determine the best methods for teaching and drilling them. For that reason, seventy drills or "methods of instruction" have been inserted and explained. Plentiful photos and photo sequences abound to better describe many of the techniques and drills explained.

Who says that an outfielder has time to think about his hitting while playing his position? If he is going to spend time thinking about his offensive game while out on the field, then sooner or later such distractions and non-involvement will undoubtedly catch up with him. There is just too much work to get done on defense to get distracted with anything else.

Having coached baseball at the high school level for the past thirty-two years, I consider myself a teacher of the game. For teaching the ins and outs of outfield play, this is the only text that I will ever need. It contains all that is required to become a truly outstanding outfielder. My hope is that *Complete Guide to Outfield Play* will become a valuable tool for the many thousands upon thousands of outfielders, would-be outfielders, and coaches who until now have been unable to find a comprehensive treatment of this subject.

Hopefully, with the help of this volume, every outfielder will soon become "outstanding in his field"!

Chapter 1

The Component Abilities
of a Great Outfielder

INTRODUCTION

To mold a baseball player into one who can truly be called "a great outfielder," hitting for average and hitting with power would certainly be among the ingredients included. However, those are offensive skills. This book, and this chapter in particular, has been written from a defensive perspective. With that viewpoint in mind, the talents essential to the great outfielder fall into the two categories of (1) natural and (2) improvable abilities. This chapter carefully defines those talents and includes a listing and short description of each.

NATURAL ABILITIES

Into the first category fall those God-given, natural abilities that no player or coach can hope to improve significantly. Either the player has them or he doesn't. For playing the outfield, there are two such natural abilities. The first is speed, and the second is a strong arm.

Speed

Great speed is needed in the outfield because of the great expanse of territory to cover. The outfield grass in a major league ballpark with foul poles 350 feet from the plate comprises about 88 percent of fair territory. Because many outfielders lack this gift of burning speed, better positioning and quicker starts are techniques that take on added importance. While both of these can be learned and improved, sheer speed is a natural, inherited ability.

A Strong Arm

Although infielders are taught to gauge the probable strength of the relay throws from outfielders and then set up accordingly, that first throw will often be in the 150–200 foot range. This distance is far greater than the 127-foot throw made by the catcher to second base. Furthermore, the movement of the baserunner(s) does not afford the luxury of a "lollipop" toss that slowly arches its way down to the relay man or base. The throw must be a "rope." Again, this amounts to an innate ability, which the best of intentions and efforts can do little about.

IMPROVABLE ABILITIES

For the player having less than great speed or something other than a "gun of an arm," there is some good news. It is this: All the other ingredients going into the makeup of a great outfielder are "improvable" abilities. That is, they are fundamentals that can be learned and improved through drill and repetition. To teach these proper mechanics and strategy does require a patient and knowledgeable coach. To learn them requires a totally dedicated ballplayer. Hopefully, this book will help with an explanation of these proper mechanics, insights, and strategies so necessary in molding great outfielders. In later chapters, much is said about each of these improvable abilities, which total nine. For now, a brief mention of each is provided.

Mental and Physical Pre-Game Readiness

To perform at one's maximum level, both the mind and body must be thoroughly lubricated for what is about to be encountered in the game. The body must be properly tuned through stretching exercises, running, and the benefits derived through a well-executed drill of playing catch. In addition, the body must be equipped with something more than just a good glove. The many kinds of plays that outfielders may be called on to make in the game must be sufficiently drilled as part of the team's pre-game infield-outfield routine. Finally, the outfielder must feel good about himself and his position. Through a proper understanding of that position, the encouragement of his coach and teammates, and his own self-motivation, he must become "pumped" to play to his potential.

Positioning

By far, this is the ability needing the greatest study and coaching. Studying both environmental and strategic positioning factors places the outfielder in the most logical position from which to await the batter's swing. As is discussed later, positioning is influenced by several factors, a few of which include weather conditions, ballpark layout, the type of pitch, the count, and the peculiarities of both the batter and the pitcher. Chapters 3 and 4 are devoted to this study along with backup responsibilities.

Getting a Good Jump on the Ball

A good stance along with correct technique in moving forward, back, or laterally greatly reduces the time needed to get to a ball regardless of the outfielder's speed or lack of it. Getting to fly balls quicker also allows the outfielder to better position his body for the upcoming throw. This is a skill that every player can master, especially through the guiding hand of his coach and the help of some well-founded tips and drills.

Judging Fly Balls

While practiced a lot, this skill can be even better perfected when practiced under very sunny or windy conditions. These are the very same conditions that outfielders so often blame for their failure to make a catch. Judging line drives, too, can improve only when players and coaches incorporate such fungo hits into their drills along with the required techniques to better these skills.

Communication With Infielders and Outfielders

So often, it is the coach who is quick to blame his players when a ball drops due to a lack of good communication. Yet, it is often the coach at fault for failing to adopt a uniform team method for calling for popups and fly balls, especially those tough "in-betweeners." He must also carefully and completely detail backup roles and responsibilities for each of the three outfield positions. In this way, outfielders and infielders alike become far more assured each time they move toward a fly ball or a deep popup. Further, outfielders will feel a greater sense of confidence in deciding their next positioning move when a play begins to unfold away from their own position.

Fielding Hits

Just as infielders need constant practice with their ground balls and do, indeed, improve, so too will the outfielders. In fact, outfielders must practice not only the standard "infield" method for going down for a ball along the ground, but also must master the one-knee and one-handed scoop methods for the times when these methods are warranted. Time must be taken to learn not only the techniques involved but the rationale leading to the decision of when to use each method.

Throwing Mechanics and Accuracy

Strength of arm, unfortunately, is no guarantee of a good throw. Correct technique is the determining factor in producing a well-thrown, accurate toss. It takes only about a second to get rid of the ball after a catch, but the mechanics that take place during that second will determine the accuracy of that throw. However, just as a pitcher's control can be improved with coaching, so can the accuracy of the outfielder's throws.

Developing Throwing Strategies

Knowing when to try to cut down a lead runner, and when instead to concentrate on a back runner or batter-runner is the mark of a knowledge-able and mature outfielder. Like the great Yankee outfielder of the past, Tommy Henrich, said, "Catching a fly ball is a pleasure, but knowing what to do with it after you catch it is a business." This, indeed, is a skill that can be taught, learned, and drilled and, therefore, improved.

Concentration

Because more action takes place in the infield, it is easy for outfielders to get lazy and begin daydreaming. In this state, such outfielders, when called upon to react to a hit ball, will often get a late start, be out of position, or will throw to a wrong base. The solution lies in becoming aware of the importance and many nuances of the outfielder's under-coached and often neglected position. Specialized outfield drills of one type or another should be scheduled into every practice session. Out-fielders should be made to feel almost overwhelmed by all of the techniques and strategies that are out there to master. Certainly an outfielder made acutely conscious of his many responsibilities will seldom be found lacking concentration during a game.

Recapping, then, here is a last look at the total of eleven abilities present in the truly outstanding outfielder.

Natural Abilities	Improvable Abilities
1. Speed	1. Mental and physical pre-game readiness
2. A strong arm	2. Positioning
	3. Getting a good jump on the ball

4. Judging fly balls
5. Communication with infielders and outfielders
6. Fielding hits
7. Throwing mechanics and accuracy
8. Developing throwing strategies
9. Concentration

This list, then, demonstrates to the outfielder with gifted speed and a strong arm that he can, indeed, become an outstanding outfielder if he is willing to put in the necessary study and practice time to master the nine improvable abilities. Further, with nine of these eleven abilities attainable by everyone, it proves that great outfielders are more often made than born. Yet, because the other two components of speed and a strong arm are inborn, it can also be said that while the outfield may be the easiest position to play, it is also perhaps the most difficult position to play well.

But what about those without great speed or a great arm, or even both? Must they write off their hopes of a future in the outfield? Most definitely not! Many have worked hard to become proficient in the nine improvable abilities and have found their efforts well rewarded. In fact, there are a number of players in the major leagues today playing the outfield with average speed or arm. How did they get there? One reason may have been their ability to hit. The other reason lies in the particular outfield position they came to play. While a strong arm and speed will never hurt an outfielder, lacking one or both of these talents is felt less at some outfield positions than others.

CHARACTERISTICS OF THE THREE
OUTFIELD POSITIONS

The Left Fielder

Although a speedy, strong-armed outfielder may be a nice fixture to have planted in left field, seldom are such players found there because of their greater need elsewhere. The fleet-footed left fielder so often gets moved to center field while the strong-armed left fielder eventually is shifted to right field.

The left fielder has neither the most ground to cover nor the longest throw to make; he is usually considered to be the least challenged of the three outfielders. Consequently, the left fielder is often found to be the least defensive-talented of the three outfielders. But is it really the least-challenging position? After all, there are many line drives and fly balls that come out that way, many of which tend to curve toward the foul line. Further, the left fielder must be able to field base hits well since so many come his way off the bats of the predominantly right-handed lineup. The right-handed batters have a tendency, as would be expected, to hit to the left half of the diamond more so than to the right.

The play at the plate is certainly one of the most important for the left fielder. Because the majority of hitters are right-handed, more of these plays at the plate are seen coming from left field than from right. Not even the center fielder, because of his usually longer throw, will have as many such plays at the plate. Besides the propensity of so many right-handed batters to pull the ball to left field, there is still another reason for these many chances for the left fielder.

The right-handed batter is often called on to hit to right field on a hit-and-run play with a runner on first. However, with a runner on second, right-handed batters are more apt to pull the ball than the left-handers, who will just as often try to slap the ball to the left side as they will try to pull the ball to the right. Left-handed batters understand the strategic geography of the infield. They understand their increased chances of beating out a hit slapped on the ground to the left side of the diamond. With this greater desire to hit the opposite way, more of their hits will fall into the range of the left fielder than will the base hits of the right-handed hitters fall to right field. As a result, with a runner on second, such hits provide even more opportunities for the left fielder to throw out a runner at the plate.

The left fielder should preferably be right-handed so that with balls hit down the line he can easily round the ball and be facing the general direction of second base as he fields the ball. This is unlike the left-handed outfielder who must first stop and pivot to be facing second base when making the throw. While a technique called the reverse pivot may be more efficient and quicker for the left-hander in this situation, it is not a method to be used matter-of-factly. Similarly, a left-handed left fielder who sprints into left-center field must reach across his body to snare a fly ball. Preferably, this type of fly ball is handled by an outfielder with a glove on his left hand, namely, a right-handed left fielder.

The Center Fielder

Usually termed "captain" of the outfield, this player must be a take-charge guy who commands the respect of his other outfielders. He should also be the fastest outfielder due to the great expanse he must cover. At this position, the emphasis is on speed more so than arm strength. Because he has to call the shots and has priority on most balls hit to left-center and right-center, the take-charge characteristic is a must. Therefore, speed and determination must be the highest priorities on the list when selecting a center fielder. Tentativeness and timidity along with a lack of speed would be at the bottom of the list. Since there is seldom any slice on balls hit to center, fly balls and line drives are the easiest to catch from this position. In addition, walls and fences aren't as much of a problem for the center fielder as they are for his flank outfielders. Bear in mind, too, that only the center fielder is able to see from his position whether each pitch is inside or outside, thus providing still one more tool in getting a jump on the ball. This is an advantage not shared with the other outfielders.

With speed in center field, the position can be played shallow in most game situations, thus taking away a lot of liners that would otherwise fall in for hits. As one might expect, there is no special advantage in the center fielder being left- or right-handed.

The Right Fielder

We remember him well, back in our days of sandlot games in which he was the last player picked. He was sent out to right where few balls were expected to be hit and where, therefore, he would be expected to do the least amount of damage. Quite often, his deficiencies included being slow and perhaps a bit overweight, too. Usually, his arm left something to be desired. However, as the level of baseball increases, so do our expectations of the skills of this key outfielder.

He should ideally have the strongest arm of the three outfielders due to the necessity for throwing to third base. This might occur when a batter tries for a triple or when a runner attempts to move from first to third on a single. This is surely one of the toughest plays for the right fielder. Even an accurate throw in this situation won't help much unless accompanied by such a strong throw that it will carry for all but one hop of the necessary distance. The shortstop, who acts as the cut-man on this play, is just that...a cut-man. Time rarely allows him to relay such throws on to third in time for a putout.

Whenever a right fielder can hold the advance of a runner from first to just one base following a base hit, it provides his team with a first and second situation, one that provides for several force-out or double-play possibilities. However, when the runner from first is able to successfully challenge the right-fielder's arm as he advances to third and the hitter to second, it leaves no force-out or double-play possibilities. Instead, it becomes a second and third situation. Two runners are now in scoring position compared to one in the first scenario. That's quite a difference. No wonder that former major league outfielder Dwight Evans has stated that he derives the same good feeling from making a fine throw as from hitting a homer.

What the right fielder really wants to do is develop a reputation around the league for his strong arm. This way, fewer coaches will chance waving their runners on for an extra base advance to third on these plays. In amateur ball, where ballplayers may not know each other as well, such reputation must be earned quickly during the pre-game outfield drills when the opposition is sure to be watching. This is the time to show off the "gun arm."

While all the outfielders must battle the shadows of twilight, it is the right fielder who must contend with the sun more so than his fellow outfielders due to the layout of most ballparks. The vast majority of major league ballparks are positioned to find the right fielder facing west and, in so doing, looking into the bright afternoon sun and, a few hours later, into the setting sun. While fewer amateur ballparks are constructed with this geographical consideration in mind, feasibility remains the determining factor.

Still another unique feature of playing right field is found in the trajectory of fly balls and line drives. While such balls will usually slice and hook toward the foul lines in both left and right fields, the degree of hook or slice is usually greater in right field. The reason for this phenomenon lies in the preponderance of right-handed pitchers and right-handed batters. From a batter's viewpoint, the pitch is moving in toward the plate from a left-to-right direction when thrown by a right-handed pitcher. For the left-handed pitcher, this would be a right-to-left direction. While some batters will fight off an inside pitch with an inside-out swing (left to right for the right-handed batter and right to left for the left-handed batter), most swings are outside-in. An outside-in swing is a right-to-left swing for the right-handed batter and left-to-right for the left-handed batter.

When the angle of pitch and the angle of swing are opposites, the tendency of the ball to slice or hook will be somewhat minimized. However, when the angles of pitch and swing are the same, then a far more wicked hook or bananalike slice may be expected. When left-handed batters face the preponderantly right-handed pitchers, this common angle of pitch and hit is created. The resulting hook can cause fits for the right fielder. When bouncing off a fence or wall, the existing spin on the ball can also make it react crazily unlike the center-field rebound. It's no wonder that a coach will want to fill that number nine position with a sure-gloved outfielder.

Because both these fly balls and hits have a tendency to slice toward the foul line or be pulled there, the advantage is to have a left-hander play the position. He will be in a better position to get the ball back into the infield quickly and efficiently on base hits fielded to his left side. Remember that this is the opposite situation to the one mentioned earlier that gave the nod to placing a right-hander in left field. If a choice must be made, though, it's usually better to place a strong-armed right-hander in right field than a left-hander with an average arm. The quality and assets of the team's other outfielders will also affect this decision.

Another exception to the rule can be applied whenever right field is a particularly bad sun field or has much larger dimensions due to a nonsymmetrical outfield layout. In this situation, the fastest outfielder might well be moved into this position even at the expense of a lesser arm.

DRILLS AND METHODS OF INSTRUCTION

Later, several indoor and outdoor drills are mentioned in connection with the nine improvable skills as these skills are discussed. For now, though, the coach has two tasks.

First, with your team picked and knowing your outfielders, you must inventory the natural assets of speed and arm strength found in each of them. While you cannot allow your thoughts to become "set in stone," you can at least begin to play with some ideas in determining your best defensive outfield.

Stopwatch clockings may be used to make speed comparisons, but findings should be tempered with the reminder that getting a good jump on the ball is just as important as sheer speed. It's not a strict matter of who is the fastest but who can get to the ball the fastest. Those two qualities are not always found in the same outfielder.

Second, the outfielders must be lectured on the eleven skills mentioned in this chapter. They must be told of the important dichotomy of natural versus improvable abilities. This makes clear to the players what will be expected of them. Further, a discussion of the characteristics found in each of the three outfielders will greatly help them understand the coach's decisions in setting his outfield. Remember, if left to the outfielders themselves, almost everyone will show a preference for playing the glamorous center-field position. However, an explanation of the skills needed there will have a sobering effect on their preconceived notions and will produce more realistic and prudent choices.

Chapter 2

Physical and Mental Preparation to Taking the Field

INTRODUCTION

To play well in a game, the outfielder must engage in a comprehensive preparation. This routine will take on many facets, some physical, but also some mental. First, there are the material tools taken out to the position. When of good quality and used as intended, these tools will certainly enhance performance. They number only four: glove, sunglasses, cap, and spikes, but their importance can't be overlooked.

Next, there is the physical preparation that must be made into a ritual before each practice and game. It consists of some calisthenics and running designed to prepare the body, but especially the legs, to perform at its maximum. To get the body ready, this phase of preparation must be taken seriously and performed conscientiously. Physical preparation also includes playing catch before the game to prepare the arm for, perhaps, some very critical upcoming throws. A simple ritual...yes, but there is a right way and a wrong way. Using some commonsense techniques in this important drill will better aid the preparation.

Physical pre-game preparation continues with the many ground balls, fly balls, and throws allotted each outfielder in the pre-game infield-outfield practice routine. Every team seems to do it differently, but the more efficiently run routines can not only prepare the players but also provide the team with some psychological one-upmanship.

Hopefully, long before game day mental and psychological preparation will have begun through a strong and growing infusion of pride in the outfield position. Unfortunately, outfielders have often felt a kind of inferiority complex about their position. This shouldn't be. Pride in the position and cohesiveness among the team's outfielders should get its start through the appointment and leadership of both an outfield captain and an outfield coach. Both will help provide a very unifying influence.

Lastly, there is the intensity that the great outfielder must continue to demonstrate even when the ball is not in play. This can be shown especially in the movement to and from his position each inning as well as in his pre-inning preparation.

Let's look at each of these now in greater detail.

THE OUTFIELDER'S TOOLS OF HIS TRADE

As shown in Photo 2-1, the outfielder has four "tools"—gloves, sunglasses, cap, and spikes.

The Glove

This should be a long-fingered glove broken-in lengthwise rather than from fingertips to heel, like the infielders' gloves. The thumb should easily make contact with the little finger of the glove. The bigger the glove, the better. Unlike the infielder, there should be no concern for the ball falling deep into the pocket of the glove. After all, the first priority is to catch the ball and, certainly, a big glove helps accomplish that end.

A new glove should never be used in a game. First, it must be sufficiently broken-in during the team practices after it has been well oiled. This could take several days, but it doesn't make sense to take a new glove into a ball game and see an easy fly ball pop out needlessly.

PHOTO 2-1: Tools of His Trade
The outfielder's basic tools are his glove, sunglasses and eye blackener, cap, and spikes.

Sunglasses and Eye Blackener

A serious outfielder will invest in a pair of flip-down sunglasses or at least a tube of eye blackener to diminish the effect of the sun's glare and then use one or both whenever conditions warrant. The outfield coach should insist on the glasses being worn during practice on sunny days. Further, the coach must find time in practice to detail the proper techniques involved with their use. These are discussed in Chapter 6. This is so often overlooked during the season. Coaches cannot assume that players are aware of the proper method of tracking fly balls in the sun with sunglasses. Players should not be expected to invest in a pair of sunglasses if the coach doesn't stress their importance through instruction and drilling in their use.

Cap

The cap is taken for granted as part of the uniform but is seldom thought of as a defensive aid for the outfielder. But, really, it is. It must be adjusted to remain on the head while charging after a ball. This way, the cap can serve the function for which it was intended, especially on sunny days. A cap that flies off the outfielder's head as he begins the chase of a fly ball is useless. If the cap is the non-adjustable type, then proper size is of greatest importance.

Spikes

Not only should spikes be worn to provide maximum traction, but those spikes should be metal whenever league rules allow. Further, when possible, spikes with replaceable cleats should be purchased to provide continued maximum traction. Cleats that are worn down defeat the purpose for which the spikes were intended. For the same reason, spikes should not be worn when walking on paved surfaces unless absolutely necessary. It's the fastest way to wear down the cleats.

PHYSICAL PRE-GAME PREPARATION

Outfielders, like all other ballplayers, must prepare their arms for throwing, their legs for running, and their bodies in general for all the twisting and stretching that a game may demand. Those of school age may have spent the greater part of the day crunched in a school desk. The pre-game throwing, stretching, running, and infield-outfield practice will prepare the body for that day's game.

Stretching

Upon arrival at the field and with spikes now laced, the player's first order of business is to stretch. Some teams perform stretching and cals together in a set routine. Other coaches allow their players the independence to stretch on their own with what exercises work best for them. What's important is that a sufficient number of proper stretching exercises be incorporated to stretch the quadriceps, hamstrings, and groin area. These are the leg areas that generally "pop" when they are pushed to their limits without sufficient warm-up.

One of the best stretching exercises for the thighs (quadriceps) is known as the Hurdler's Stretch (Photo 2-2). Sit on the ground with one leg tucked back while the other is extended forward. Then, slowly lower yourself backward until the back is in contact with the ground. The flatter the body, the more the quadriceps will stretch. After 15 seconds, reverse the leg positions.

An example of a good exercise for the hamstrings, located on the backside of the thighs, is one performed in a standing position. Begin by placing the right foot immediately to the *left* of the left foot. Then, without allowing any bend in the knees, bend at the waist until the fingertips of both hands contact the ankle (or beyond if possible) of the right leg (Photo 2-3). No bouncing should take place. Once this position is achieved, hold it for ten seconds before reversing the legs. During this period, the lactic acid disturbed within the muscle will cause some discomfort behind the knee, but will quickly disappear upon reassuming an erect position.

To stretch the groin area, a Yoga-type of exercise is suggested in which a sitting position is taken. Reaching out with both hands, grasp the instep area of each foot, place the feet sole to sole, and move them in

PHOTO 2-2: Hurdler's Stretch
The flatter the back, the greater the stretch of the quadricep muscle.

PHOTO 2-3: Hamstring Stretch
To achieve maximum stretching, neither knee should bend.

toward the groin area while remaining in the sitting position. Moving the feet in will not cause much stretching, but what will is a maximum bending forward at the waist (Photo 2-4). Fifteen seconds of this exercise should suffice.

These are just three of the numerous exercises designed to accomplish these muscle stretchings and are only suggestions. Others with which the

PHOTO 2-4: Groin Stretch
With hands clasped around the feet, the outfielder leans his upper body forward, lowering the elbows as close to the ground as possible.

players are familiar and comfortable should be added or substituted. What's really important is to realize that just as the arm is the pitcher's "bread and butter," the outfielder's arm *and* legs are his dual "bread and butter." When finished, some running in the outfield grass should get all the "juices" flowing. Time will often dictate the amount of running, but two full jogs from one baseline around to the other in left and right field should be a minimum to really getting those legs stretched out. The final 150 feet of each romp across the outfield should be sprinted.

Playing Catch

To prepare the arm, the outfielder will want to get in some "catch." However, a good lead-in is a quick stretching exercise called "hanging around" (Photo 2-5). Using a dugout roof, fence, or backstop, grab on as high as possible and then allow the body to stretch by hanging. Of course, with the greatest amount of stretching taking place in the shoulder area and spinal column, what better way could there be to ready the arm and shoulder for some catch?

All catch should be played off the infield grass and away from the dugout. The best place is on the outfield grass with all throws being made in parallel fashion for obvious safety reasons.

PHOTO 2-5: "Hanging Around"
This is an excellent shoulder- and spine-loosening exercise performed prior to playing catch.

Because catchers must "short arm" their snap throws, and because most infielders throw "three-quarters," it is wise for outfielders to play catch only with other outfielders. Otherwise, bad throwing habits can develop unconsciously just through catch with these non-outfielder partners. Furthermore, since outfielders have the longest throws to make, they should want to throw only with others who also must prepare to make long throws.

All catch should begin at short distances of about 45 feet, with the distance between players increasing only when the upper arms and shoulders feel loose and ready for it.

Unnecessary talk and storytelling have no place at this time when players need concentration to produce maximum results. Even with something as simple as playing catch, a number of very important techniques must be incorporated to gain maximum power, control, and distance.

To begin, the ball is gripped across the seams for best control. Then, the throwing arm is allowed to follow its full range of motion by passing the palm down and past the thigh with the wrist turned slightly to the outside. As the hand comes back, the arm is extended to its greatest length with the fingers remaining on top of the ball all the while.

A high elbow is the key to getting on top of the ball. Lowering the throwing elbow causes the two fingers atop the ball to angle from their proper 12-o'clock position to about a 2-o'clock position. This reduces maximum power. Outfielders must make all throws directly overhand to produce the greatest possible "carry."

Then the movement forward to complete the throwing action takes place. The glove hand helps produce power and leverage for the throwing hand by pointing out toward the target as the throwing arm rears back. The ball should never be thrown with the glove arm down at the side, nor should a ball be thrown without a precise target in mind.

At the moment the throwing arm is fully extended back with ball in hand, the front shoulder must be closed. That means that if a make-pretend bar connected the two shoulders, the front end of that bar, if extended, would point directly at the target for at least a split second. Failure to close this front shoulder to its maximum reduces the slingshot effect that takes place when this same front shoulder reopens. This is the same movement that occurs during a pitcher's leg kick when he rotates his leg, hip, and shoulder back to a coil-like position for a maximum forward thrust.

When the ball is released, it is a loose wrist rather than a tight grip that is propelling the ball. A tight grip only leads to a tensed arm that will adversely affect control. Every toss should be smooth and loose.

As the ball is thrown, the foot on the side of the throwing arm must be lifted, not dragged. It rocks forward about two feet before swinging

PHOTO SERIES 2-6: Playing Catch

The ball begins its full range of motion route, passing near the rear hip. The throwing arm is then extended back with fingers atop the ball. The shoulders are level and in line with the target where the glove is also pointed for leverage. The high elbow passes the ear just ahead of the hand as the near-completed weight shift leads into the snap release. As the ball is released, the thrower's bent back leg rocks forward just slightly beyond the left knee and back again while one to two inches off the ground.

(a)

(b)

(c)

(d)

back. It is also an inch or two off the ground at this time with the cleats up just high enough to clear the turf. Meanwhile, the knee of that leg rocks forward and up to or just past the other knee (Photo Series 2-6).

When the weight shift of the throwing action occurs, the resulting force falling upon the lead leg must find its way to an open front foot, not one that's completely closed. Such a closed front foot only locks the hips, thus reducing the power behind the throw.

In playing catch, outfielders should never shortchange themselves by throwing to their partner from a maximum of 90 feet or less. Although the throwing distance may begin at about 45 feet, the period of playing catch should not conclude until that distance has been lengthened to at least 120 feet. Completing five to ten of these throws at this maximum distance should conclude the warm-up catch. No one should continue playing catch without a goal in mind other than to continue playing until called in by the coach. The purpose of playing catch is to stretch and warm up the arm, and when that has been accomplished, the catch should stop.

Infield-Outfield Pre-Game Practice

Shortly afterward, it becomes time for the infield-outfield pre-game practice routine to begin. Its main purpose once again is to provide the feeling of those ground balls, fly balls, and the many different throws often required in game situations. It will also get the outfielders adjusted to the peculiarities of the field conditions along with such weather factors that day as sun, wind, turf texture, and moistness.

Unfortunately for outfielders, there are still too many teams using the time-wasting one-ball-at-a-time approach. Although safety must be considered, this approach doesn't prepare players very efficiently. Basically, what happens here is that the coach hits one ball to one player and allows the play to be completed before hitting the next ball. This amounts to a player being hit one ball out of every eight (not nine, since the pitcher rarely participates). This number can at least be quadrupled in the same amount of time through the use of one form or another of a routine known as the Kamikaze Drill.

In the space of five minutes, each outfielder will be fungoed 12 to 15 balls. That gives him the opportunity to make four or five hard throws to each of the bases.

There are three phases to this drill. Besides the three outfielders, a complete infield is needed along with an extra infielder needed on the outfield grass between second and third. The coach and one assistant handle the fungo hitting, with each using a non-starting player to "retrieve" incoming tosses from the infielders. The two fungo hitters and their retrievers stand on opposite sides of the pitcher's mound. The extra infielder functions as the relay man for the left-fielder's throw to third base in Phase I. Then, he becomes the relay man for the left-fielder's throw to second base in Phase II. Finally, in Phase III, he becomes the relay man for the center-fielder's throw to third base.

Beginning with Phase I, the coach, standing on the third-base side of the mound, alternately but continuously hits to the left and center fielders. Included is a balanced mixture of fly balls and base hits. His assistant hits solely to the right fielder. In this phase, the left fielder makes his throws into third base with the extra infielder positioning himself in the cutoff position as the shortstop normally would. The center fielder makes his throws into second base with the second baseman at the base and with the shortstop in a relay position for the throw. Meanwhile, the right fielder is making his throws into the plate with the first baseman in the cut position. Although three balls are in motion simultaneously, this is the simplest of the three phases, because none of the throws is criss-crossing. Each phase requires no more than 1½ minutes. This will complete all three phases within five minutes.

Before Phase II is described, see Diagram 2-1 and study the direction of the balls coming off the bat (solid lines) and the outfielders' throws into the bases (dashed lines). Note that each fungo hitter will have a player

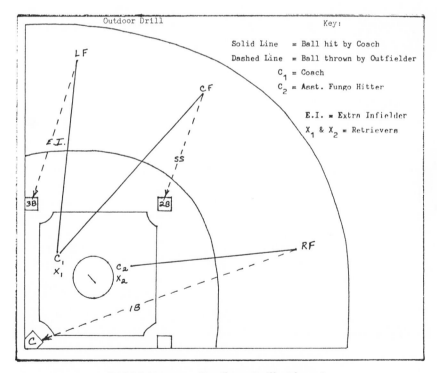

DIAGRAM 2-1: Kamikaze Drill - Phase I
With none of the outfielders' throws criss-crossing, this phase is the
easiest to master.

standing behind him retrieving the throws from the infielders (denoted by X_1 and X_2). "E.I." denotes the needed extra infielder.

When the coach is ready to move on to Phase II, he calls out "Switch!" During practice, the coach walks through the mechanics of each phase very slowly with all his players. He must make sure that the "lines of flight" of both the "hit" and the "thrown" balls are left vacated by those not involved in that part of the drill. Remember that not one or two, but three balls will be in constant motion once the drill begins. Players must also be cautioned in their retrieval of balls that may skip away from their intended flight or that may have been sent "off-line" by the fungo hitter. Nowhere is this more important than in Phase II, which contains the greatest number of thrown balls criss-crossing (Diagram 2-2).

This time, the left fielder throws to second base, with the extra infielder in the cut position. The center fielder will throw home with the first baseman taking the relay from a position on the far side of the mound. To do this, the positions of the two fungo hitters and their retrievers must

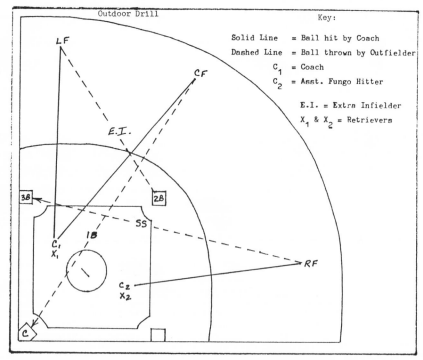

DIAGRAM 2-2:   Kamikaze Drill - Phase II
Safety and caution take a high priority in this phase since not just one, but two sets of throws criss-cross.

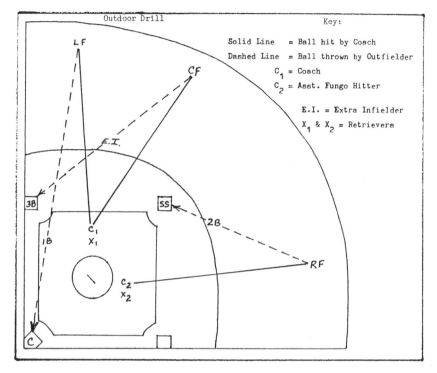

DIAGRAM 2-3: Kamikaze Drill - Phase III
In this phase, the coach and his retriever move to the shortstop side of the
mound to clear the way for the left fielder's throw to the plate.

be altered slightly for safety precautions. Note the changes in Diagram 2-2.
Meanwhile, the right fielder is practicing his toughest throw to third base.
The shortstop sets up in a direct line between the right fielder and the
third base bag in assuming his cut position. Studying the diagram for
Phase II of the Kamikaze Drill with its multi-crisscrossing attests to its
well-picked name. Its name also emphasizes the caution to be shown in
both the initial instruction and the actual execution of the drill.

　　　When the time is right to move on to the third and final phase of the
Kamikaze Drill, the coach again calls out, "Switch!"

　　　In this phase, the left fielder throws home while the center fielder
throws to third, and the right fielder makes his shortest throw to second.
This time, the second baseman will assume the cut position for the right-
fielder's throw to second while the shortstop takes the throw at the base.
Meanwhile, the extra infielder positions himself for the cut for the throw
from the center fielder to the third baseman at the bag. This creates one
slightly unrealistic game situation. Whereas the third baseman would

normally assume the cut position for the left-fielder's throw to the plate, this responsibility is given to the first baseman. It is the first baseman, then, who sets up in the cut position for all of the throws to the plate in this drill. Although the assistant fungo hitter may remain at the right side of the mound, the main fungo hitter must move to the shortstop side of the mound to vacate the line of flight for the left-fielder's throw to the plate (Diagram 2-3).

With frequent use, the Kamikaze Drill or one of its many variations will soon become one of maximum efficiency, finesse, and fun. Practiced to perfection, it will provide the outfielders with a great pre-game tune-up. It will also help instill in all the outfielders a close identity with their position.

OUTFIELD COACHING AND LEADERSHIP

An outfield captain should be appointed. Usually a starter, and often the center fielder, he can help unite all the outfielders, not just the starters, to a common purpose. He can keep them up during the game, see that they move according to the count and other circumstances, and help in practice with many of the outfield drills. This kind of leadership is often overlooked but will pay great dividends over the course of the season. In addition, it lends credence to the importance the coach places in the role of his outfielders.

As great a job as he may try to do, the outfield captain, being a player himself, cannot be expected to take full responsibility for the outfielders. So, unless the head coach can handle the job himself, he should appoint an assistant coach to oversee all outfield matters. He'll design, direct, and critique drills. He'll work with all the outfielders during the practices and will oversee their actions during the games. This specialized coach will work to instill cohesiveness and pride in his charges, constantly "pushing" the importance of their role in the team's success. After all, they do comprise one-third of the starting defensive team.

However, this outfield coach along with the head coach will also kick any outfielder in the pants when he is deserving. He will emphasize that outfielders are part of the last line of defense, and for that reason, he will never accept excuses when it comes to wind, sun, field conditions, or communication problems. Soon, this preaching will transform into a self-pride among the outfielders. Today, that's a rarity with most teams, where outfielders suffer from an identity crisis due to the neglect shown to their position. Outfield coaches and captains will greatly help in reversing this undesirable attitude.

Outfielders must come to believe that no pitcher, catcher, or infielder could ever do the job they do without just as much training and hard work.

So often outfielders are shuffled off to the side, especially in practice. But now the outfield coach will see to it that this does not happen. Instead, along with the outfield captain, the outfield coach will be constantly on hand to help develop, and then maintain, a very positive mental attitude and self-image.

PRIDE AND INTENSITY

Before and during every game, the outfielder must continue to demonstrate just how psyched and into the game he is. He wants to place his well-tuned self-image as an outfielder on parade. This kind of pride and intensity can be demonstrated in four special ways.

First, there is the sprint to and from his position. He doesn't stop until reaching the edge of the dugout or the area where he plans to position himself for the first pitch of the inning. This lets the opposition know just how into the game he is as well as the extent to which he is looking for a chance to contribute to their defeat. It demonstrates his desire to display his skills toward a winning cause. He is mentally keyed to respond instantly to each situation as it develops. There is no lack of concentration with him. He is aware of the total game situation, not just the score. He is once again showing his pride, love, and intensity for the outfield position. He is truly ready for any challenge that may come his way.

Second, to be prepared to sprint onto the field each inning without hesitation, the three starting outfielders will keep their gloves together in the dugout along with a ball in the glove of the outfield captain. Any outfielder left on base is quickly "picked up" by one of his outfield teammates. The outfield captain places a ball in his glove each time he comes into the dugout from his position. This way, there is no searching for a warm-up ball each inning when taking the field.

During the pre-inning warm-ups, catch should be played with full intensity. The two most distant outfielders play catch while the nearest throws with a fourth outfielder stationed in foul territory about 120 feet from the plate. Consider that even with just five hard throws made before each inning, this will total 35 by game's end! This can be called "preventive maintenance." It is important that all of those throws are hard and overhand. Lofting meaningless, short flies is never appropriate unless the sun is playing a factor that day.

Finally, the catch of a fly ball anytime during the game is an opportunity to exhibit pride, intensity, and arm strength with a serious and hard throw back in toward the middle infielder taking the throw. The outfielder's time to rest and let up will come only after the last out of the game. And he wouldn't have it any other way! Whether his team wins or loses, he will have just played the whole game psyched from start to finish and showed it every chance he got.

DRILLS AND METHODS OF INSTRUCTION

Teaching the kinds of game preparation and intangibles of pride and intensity discussed in this chapter is best accomplished indoors. A classroom talk to the outfielders is a good setting in which to point out the importance of the outfielders' four tools of his trade. There, too, the philosophy behind the appointment of an outfield coach and captain can be made clear. The person serving as outfield coach can be introduced, and the outfield captain can be named as well.

In this kind of atmosphere, too, the head coach or the outfield coach can spell out the ingredients for pride and intensity in an outfielder. He must really sell these points.

A session in the gym provides a good opportunity to explain the team's routine for stretching. A demonstration will serve to reinforce the proper execution of these exercises, especially if the team members are going to be left to design their own pre-game stretching routine.

Out on the field, the logistics and techniques for playing catch are explained, with special attention drawn to those items peculiar to the outfielders. Although the techniques for throwing a baseball can be taught indoors, the logistics and safety factors to be emphasized will have greater impact out on the field. Two special varieties of playing catch can help to convince the players of the importance of the numerous components that go into each throw. Ironically, the two drills are rather opposite each other.

The first of these drills is called the Knee Catch Drill. Performed in pairs for about five minutes, knee catch finds each participant on both knees with back straight, not slouched back on the heels. Because the normal weight transfer from back foot to front foot is impossible this way, the thrower must rely on maximum production out of the other throwing components that add up to a strong throw. This includes a grip across the seams, a high elbow, parallel shoulders, and a strong hip and trunk rotation. The grip across the seams helps with control and velocity through a strong wrist pop upon release. The parallel shoulders help to emphasize the importance of gaining leverage and power with the aid of an extended glove hand. Because the thrower's glove-side leg is locked in place, his attempt to close his front shoulder will be stunted. It will be, however, the degree of trunk rotation that will help to maximize the front shoulder closing in this limited stance drill. By asking the outfielders to practice a quick transfer of the ball from their gloves to their throwing hand, a two-handed catch will become a pleasant by-product along with a strong release pop. While the distance between players in knee catch can vary, you are wise to ask for long knee catch from the outfielders, who need to produce greater distance than the other players.

You may opt for the one-knee variation of this drill which has the throwing-side knee down, but the glove-side knee up. Here, all the mechanics of the throwing technique are made easier with the added leverage of a bent and braced left leg.

Another variety of catch designed to improve strength is a shorter two- to three-minute drill performed between pairs of outfielders from a standing position. It is called the Long Toss Drill. Using a distance between players of 120 to 200 feet or more, emphasis is placed on the proper footwork mentioned earlier along with a strong follow-through. Throwing with a loose wrist and full range of motion will help to achieve yet another objective, that of "hitting the target." That target is a chest-high toss to the long toss partner. Limited indoor facilities will prohibit many teams from utilizing this drill indoors.

Finally, as mentioned earlier, out on the field you can present a slow and clear description of the Kamikaze Drill, or whatever variation you may wish to create for the pre-game outfield warm-up. While you could have your players walk through the phases of this drill indoors, it would still need repeating outdoors to get a realistic feel for the various positionings, distances, and factors to watch for in the area of safety. Once perfected, however, this will be one drill that every player on the team, and the outfielders, in particular, will look forward to with excitement.

Outfield Positional Play: Individual Strategy

INTRODUCTION

If every outfielder knew exactly where each ball was going to be hit, he could position himself there before the pitch, and no longer would speed be vital for outfielders. That not being the case, however, he must instead consider every possible clue that could in any way forewarn him. After all, the closer an outfielder can station himself to where the ball is hit, the easier will be the play.

There are three types of factors that govern positioning. The first two might be termed "before the fact." These include both environmental and strategic factors. The third type is "after the fact" positioning, better known as backup responsibilities.

Chapters 3 and 4, however, which both deal with a study of positioning, have been subdivided using a different criterion. The decision to position a certain way may be the result of a "personal" determination based on any number of environmental and strategic factors. The outfielder's thoughts and resulting decision to play in, back, to the left or right are just that...his own. This kind of thinking is encouraged and must be an ongoing process that continues to move the outfielder around as weather conditions, pitchers, batters, score, and innings change. Such independent and personal positioning is the focus of study in Chapter 3. Later, in Chapter 4, team- and coach-conceived positioning alignments as well as team backup policies are investigated.

ENVIRONMENTAL FACTORS

Environmental factors are those that "come with the territory" for a given day and ballpark. They refer to weather conditions and ballpark makeup, especially in the case of open fields. Let's take a look at the most important of these environmental positioning clues.

The Sun

First, consider the weather. Check the sun. Will it be a factor? If so, from what angle will it influence the chase of a fly ball? It will certainly affect some outfield positions more than others, depending on the ballpark's layout and time of day. If the sun may cause problems, then sunglasses or eye blackener will be in order. How to properly use those sunglasses is discussed in Chapter 6.

The Wind

Next, check the wind for both its direction and strength. This can be done by checking leaves on a tree, observing any flags, or by the old standard means of flicking grass blades into the air. If the wind is a factor, then it will always be better to overestimate than to underestimate its force, since chasing down a ball is always more difficult than slowing up for one.

Ballpark Layout and Obstructions

Next, consider any obstructions peculiar to the ballpark. In an enclosed park, check for bullpen mounds as well as the height and structure of fences or walls along the foul line areas. Non-secured hoses or other landscaping equipment could also pose problems if located within live ball areas. While this should never be the case, occasionally it does happen. Learn where the live ball area ends in the foul territory area so that additional obstacles and obstructions are not encountered unnecessarily in areas that have been clearly ruled out of play by the ground rules. Of course, in an open field, obstructions can run the gamut, including trees, bushes, flagpoles and goalposts, sidewalks, buildings, picnic benches, and picnickers, too. Make a mental note of their whereabouts.

The Outfield Fence and Warning Track

Any outfield fences must be checked out very carefully. Check their height, proximity, construction material, and "bounceability." The latter could make the difference between winning and losing. The kind of "kick-back" that a ball takes off an outfield fence or wall can be determined by either throwing balls against it or by asking for fungoes to be hit to the wall or fence.

The size of the field should help determine playing depth. In a small ballpark, playing up close can be smart. This way, some of the loopers that might otherwise fall in for hits can be caught. Another strategy might be to take away the long shots by playing deep. Which of these strategies is used will be determined by strategic factors discussed next.

When a warning track is present, its size and surface makeup should be examined to discover the approximate number of steps from the track to the wall. Then, this information is stored for use in the game.

The Outfield Turf

Another environmental factor involves the outfield grass. Inspect it to determine whether the grass will provide a well-cushioned bounce or will it instead tend to make the ball skid upon contact. Has it been recently cut, or is it dense? On the other hand, the terrain may be bare, rocky, or even sloping. If it's bare, is it also hard? If so, decide now how base hits should be handled. It may be necessary to forego a bit of aggressiveness and opt instead for the safety of a big bounce, even if it means lying back a bit. Trying to come up with the ball on the short or in-between hop on this kind of barren field could result in the ball skipping by for needless extra bases.

For shots to left-center and right-center, it will be necessary to take a deeper angle due to the ball's greater speed. This will be the case with barren or artificial-surface outfields as well as those just having a "fast" turf. The outfielder just can't risk having the ball go all the way to the fence.

How rough the outfield is will determine the need to field base hits in the normal fashion or down on one knee for a slightly slower, but safer and surer method. It will also determine the risk in occasionally charging a ball from the side to pick up a grounder more quickly in hopes of throwing out an advancing runner.

The rougher the field, the greater the need for the outfielders to back up each other. The same is true of a wet outfield (either from rain or an early morning dew) when the grass will often lack its "cushiony" texture and instead cause the ball to skip and slide, especially upon the descent of a line drive.

STRATEGIC FACTORS

While the sun may come and go, and while wind velocity may change during the game's course, environmental factors are relatively static. Strategic factors, on the other hand, are quite another matter. They are constantly changing. The pitcher, with his strengths and weaknesses and his pitch-by-pitch selections, has a great bearing on just where the outfielders position themselves. Knowledge of the batter and recall of his previous at bats, as well as his position in the lineup should all help to influence positioning. Also important, but so often forgotten, is the influence of the constantly changing count on the batter. Consciously or subconsciously, most batters become more or less aggressive as the count moves in their favor or away. However, changing position as the count changes should be a part of the team's overall defensive strategy rather than being done independently by just one or two of the outfielders. Otherwise, big, unprotected gaps could result. Therefore, this becomes a "team" type of positioning strategy and is studied in Chapter 4.

Even the speed of the infielders and outfielders playing positions nearby can affect an outfielder's positioning.

Finally, no one can dispute the popularity of positioning dictated by score, inning, position of any runner or runners, and the number of outs. Let's take a closer look at each of these strategic factors.

Speed and Ability Level of Adjacent Players

With some speedy infielders with above-average ability playing in front of the outfielder, he can maintain a deeper position. Otherwise, he can't. Some infielders can go back on a deep popup or short fly and cover it, while others will struggle and need the outfielder's help.

This strategy also holds for adjacent outfielders. While playing a straightaway position, for instance, it might seem logical at first thought for the outfielders to position themselves an equal distance apart. However, they all have their own strengths and weaknesses, the most important of which relate to speed and quickness. A speedy center fielder, then, might care to shade to the side of a slow adjacent outfielder to better cover that half of the outfield. With a faster outfielder nearby, however, a greater gap could be left there.

Playing the Opposite Field

Unless there is reason to believe otherwise, the outfielder can often play shallow when playing the opposite field to a batter's strength. Although many young batters may hit to the opposite field, seldom will it be with power. This way, some of the soft liners lifted that way can be snared rather than dropping in for a hit. Such a shallow position, though, is ill-advised against someone known to hit with authority to the opposite field, especially a batter in the number three through six positions in the order.

Playing a Shallow Outfield Position

Most outfielders play at normal depths except, of course, when the situation dictates otherwise. However, some outfielders prefer to take a shallow position regardless of the speed and ability of their adjacent outfielders and nearby infielders. To be successful with such a philosophy, an outfielder must be gifted with the ability to go back on a ball in hawklike fashion. Playing shallow by choice is very foolhardy in an open field, but it has some merit on a closed field, especially for a center fielder. Joe DiMaggio and Tris Speaker were probably the two most famous center fielders who played shallow by choice. This way, many line drives and bloopers hit just over the heads of the infielders can be caught, and certainly, there are more of these than of the long, towering fly variety. Going back after a fly ball isn't always the very difficult play that it is thought to be. Catching the ball at eye level or higher, even though the outfielder is running away from the infield, is often much easier than trying to snare a short fly requiring a long run in toward the infield. Such knee-high or shoe-top grabs must be made with the glove up in basketlike fashion. This is one of the outfielder's tougher plays.

Also, because of the proximity involved, there are increased chances to throw out advancing runners. Of course, there are certain game situations when a deeper position is warranted to protect a lead.

From the other side of the coin, the shallow-playing center fielder is unable to cut off base hits in the alleys. This must be taken into consideration with certain defensive strategies, as when the tying run is at first with the winning run at the plate. Of course, the closer the fence, the shallower the center fielder can play. The outfielder who plays shallow can seldom make the leaping catch at the fence, because he'll never get there in time. On the other hand, if he is able to go back to the fence and wait for a semi-line drive, then he's really playing too close to the fence for someone who wants to play shallow.

However, to play shallow by choice (as opposed to some team strategic design), the center fielder must work hard in practice to learn to go back on a ball quickly. Catlike instincts, though, are the overriding criteria. Without such quickness, this positional philosophy is ill-advised. But if the center fielder does possess such gifts, the hard work can pay big dividends in the long run...no pun intended!

The Pitcher and the Pitch

Knowledge of the pitcher and his repertoire is yet another factor to consider in positioning. Even viewing the batter's stride, hips, and hands as he prepares to hit a pitch over a certain portion of the plate can provide a clue. The center fielder, especially, has a great advantage. He can see the pitch moving in over the inside or outside half of the plate or down the middle. All the outfielders can use this kind of information to get their bodies moving in the ball's most probable direction.

Having a pitcher with excellent velocity makes it tough for batters to get around on the ball. Against such pitchers, the hitters will be more apt to hit toward the opposite field. Pitchers without this burning speed will have a tendency to see more of their pitches pulled. Regardless of the pitcher's velocity, the later innings will often demonstrate the tiring effects of the game on him by way of more balls being pulled.

Outfielders will often see a number of curve balls pulled, especially curves breaking in toward the batter as when a right-handed batter faces a left-handed pitcher. These kinds of clues must be an influence in how outfielders set up for each batter.

To keep outfielders informed of each upcoming pitch, a signal system can be devised with a middle infielder. After all, only the pitcher and middle infielders should ever be able to read the catcher's signals.

One system often used is a behind-the-back closed fist to signal a fast ball, while an open hand indicates a curve, and wiggled fingers a change-up.

Another method calls for the infielder to hit his mitt once for a fast ball, hit the left thigh for a curve, or hit the right thigh for a change-up. Obviously, outfielders can't see the finger signs of the catcher, so they must rely on infielders. Knowing what pitch is coming, along with the outfielder's other positioning adjustments, can make the difference between a successful catch and a base hit, perhaps one for extra bases.

Some think that this kind of relay system takes away from the outfielder's concentration, but what it really does is to better his involvement in the game and to better position him for the upcoming pitch. No positioning adjustment, though, should be made until the pitch is on its way. Some batters are sharp enough to watch for a movement by the outfielders in one direction or the other as the pitcher is getting set to begin his windup motion. With such a premature movement by even one outfielder, the batter would be tipped off to the fast ball when seeing the outfielder shade to his opposite side. If they were to shade to his pull side, it would indicate an off-speed pitch.

Watching the batter's every move as he strides to the ball is still another tip-off. For instance, if the batter's body is seen moving toward the outside portion of the plate to hit a pitch there, chances are that the ball will be hit toward the opposite field. Consequently, the three outfielders can start moving in that direction. The reverse is true when a batter begins opening up to stride into a pitch on the inside corner. Oftentimes, a step or two gained in getting a start on the ball enables outfielders to catch balls that would otherwise fall untouched.

Positioning by the Batting Order

Sometimes, for lack of better knowledge, it might be necessary to look to a batter's position in the batting order to learn more about his hitting tendencies. When this is the case, the number one and two hitters are played straightaway. Their assets usually include the ability to make contact, but usually without a lot of power. For the middle of the lineup (#3 through #6), hitting with either some or a lot of power is usually expected. These are the R.B.I. guys. Because they are expected to show at least a little power, these players are usually played to pull the ball rather than being played straightaway. Finally, there is the bottom third of the order. Because their hitting deficiencies often include a slow bat or the trait of hitting defensively, many of the balls they hit will travel to their opposite field. Consequently, they should usually be played that way. Generally speaking, the top and bottom of the order are played at average depth or shallow. The middle-of-the-order hitters are played average to deep.

Knowledge of the Batter

It can help greatly when an upcoming batter's strengths, weaknesses, and tendencies are known. This knowledge might come from a teammate, coach, or study of previous times at bat. It might also come about through personal experience of prior competition with this player. In any case, this information can help decide whether to play deep or shallow, and whether to play to the pull or opposite field or even straightaway. Even the foul balls hit can provide information. Does the hitter swing early or late? The lunger, for example, will not hit with power, but will usually pull almost everything. He is the hitter who begins his swing simultaneously with his stride.

On the other hand, the late swinger will hit the fast ball to the opposite field. Scouting, viewing pre-game batting practice, and watching each hitter's distinctive habits throughout the game are great ways to learn this kind of valuable positioning information. All of the many positioning clues discussed in this chapter are of a personal nature to each outfielder. Each may choose to place his faith in as many or as few as he likes and to whatever degree he likes. Chapter 4 presents a number of team-designed defensive alignments and strategies in which every outfielder has a part to play.

DRILLS AND METHODS OF INSTRUCTION

How does anyone teach or drill positional play? Certainly it is not easy. For the most part, the topic doesn't seem to lend itself to what we normally think of as a drill. On the other hand, it provides an opportunity to try another approach.

Drills: Environmental Factors

The environmental factors of positional play can be very successfully taught by taking the team's set of outfielders on a "hike" and "tour" of the team's home outfield and perhaps another one as well for comparison. Just as you will often teach some aspect of base running by lecturing the team from some place on the base paths, this time you take your half dozen or so outfielders out to a position in the outfield and use this appropriate setting as your classroom backdrop. From there, discuss the environmental factors to investigate prior to taking the field. For best results, this mini-session should include discussion and questioning as well as pure lecture. Topics covered will include sun and wind, ballpark layout and obstructions, fences, turf, and any warning track. Encourage outfielders to survey these factors for each outfield position they might play, remembering too, that different weather conditions can easily change the playing condition of their home field. Subsequently, this hike and mental survey should be carried out by every outfielder before a game.

Drills: Strategic Factors

Next we have the strategic factors to positioning to teach and drill. What influence will the speed and ability level of the adjacent players have on an outfielder's positioning? The same must be asked of the outfielder's knowledge of the batter and the latter's position in the batting order. What kind of pitcher is on the mound, and what pitch is he about to throw? What should be the outfielder's thinking when playing the opposite field to a hitter's strength, and what about thoughts of adopting a shallow positioning philosophy? Such strategic factors and their influences in positioning can be taught in the classroom or, as with the environmental factors, out in the outfield for better effect.

For greatest impact, however, do not combine these two discussions. Attention spans can be short. Therefore, combining the two topics might prove to be too much for one hike.

Chapter 4

Outfield Positional Play: Team Strategy

INTRODUCTION

In positioning for a batter, decisions based upon the free and independent thinking of each outfielder, as studied in Chapter 3, are fine...up to a point. There still must exist, though, a common thread of team defensive strategy. Such strategies are known as defensive "alignments." They must be understood and ready to be set in motion at a moment's notice by way of a signal from the coach or from his onfield representative. In most cases, the outfielders will independently position as they see fit. However, sometimes the coach or infield captain will want the entire defense to be thinking alike in its plan to defense a given hitter. Therefore, when a particular alignment strategy is called, all must be ready to respond. This chapter studies six such defensive strategies.

Chapter 4 also investigates three commonsense game situations that should bring an automatic response from the outfielders in their positioning plans. Further, as part of a team concept of outfield defense and strategy, all three outfielders will be encouraged to employ an ongoing "movement-by-the-count" philosophy. These prescribed unit movements of two, four, or six steps in one direction or another are executed simultaneously by all three outfielders after every pitch. The use of this very worthwhile strategy will surely help to keep the outfielders focused and even better positioned than they otherwise would be. This strategy attempts to counteract the psychological changes in the batter's confidence level as his count changes for better or worse with every pitch. We are merely trying to play the percentages.

Finally, we close our look at positioning with a detailed list of "post-pitch" responsibilities for each of the three outfield positions. Post-pitch positioning is just another term for "backup roles and responsibilities." For an outfielder to be constantly looking for a way to help on plays that do not originate with him is the culmination of the outfielder's desire to be the best positioned outfielder he can be! He is constantly looking to help as a "Johnny on the spot!"

TEAM OUTFIELD AND INFIELD ALIGNMENTS

Although outfielders may already have several clues on which to base their positioning for each batter, so too does the coach. Often, because of his experience, the coach may wish to determine the positioning for the entire defense. He'll wish to move his outfield, and infield too, to positions that he feels will best defense both the batter and the game situation. Perhaps the concept is reminiscent of the football coach sending in a play rather than allowing the quarterback to determine his own. Certainly he will be making use of many of the very same factors that outfielders would consider if left on their own. This way, though, he will have everyone thinking alike and, by signaling for a particular defensive alignment, will have everyone playing in defensive unison.

However, unlike the football coach who sends in his thoughts and strategy through a player sent into the huddle, the baseball coach must do his communicating through a series of hand and arm signals from the dugout area. In the absence of these signals from the coach, the infield captain, usually the shortstop, is often given the freedom and responsibility of calling the same signals to move the infielders and outfielders into an alignment that he feels will best defense the hitter and the situation.

As mentioned earlier, there are so many factors to consider. There is the position of the batter in the lineup, his stance, count, previous plate appearances, and not to be forgotten, the man on the mound. Is it a power pitcher out there or perhaps one who relies a lot on off-speed pitches? Is the particular match-up of batter and pitcher one of right-handed versus left-handed, or are they both throwing and hitting from the same side? Remember, batters hitting against pitchers throwing from the opposite side get a little better look at the ball and have a tendency to pull these pitchers a bit more than they might against pitchers throwing from the same side.

The score, inning, game situation, wind, and physical makeup of the ballpark are still other considerations in determining the best defensive alignment. It is not surprising, then, that a coach may often wish to take this element of the thinking game out of the individual hands of the players and instead signal for one common defense. Of course, such positioning based on these many factors along with a little intuition and guesswork will never prove to be an exact science. Yet, they should produce better results over the course of a game than no positional strategy at all. Just plunking down on three square feet of turf and staying there for the entire game, hoping for the best, is just that...no strategy!

Just how many defenses will be defined and what names and signals they will go by will vary, of course, but six should cover most situations and batters.

Let's take them one at a time. For each defensive alignment, we'll assign a name and signal and determine just when such a defense may be in order. In addition, the defensive placement of each player will be mentioned.

1. Straightaway Defensive Alignment
(Diagram 4-1)

The coach signals this defense by raising both arms straight up over his head just like the football referee signaling a converted point after a

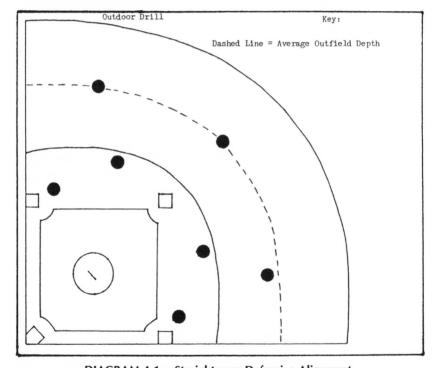

DIAGRAM 4-1:   Straightaway Defensive Alignment
This alignment assumes a right-handed batter, since the right fielder is playing slightly shallower than the other two outfielders. Otherwise, the left fielder would assume this shallower position for a left-handed batter.

touchdown. This alignment finds each player positioning himself in his most "usual" position. This is the best defense to use when the batter is known to be a spray hitter who uses the whole field. For this reason, he must be played "honest." The straightaway defense might also be dubbed "The Dummy Defense" since it will also be used often against a hitter about whom the coach has little available information. The center fielder along with the outfielder playing to the batter's pull side will play at medium depth, while the outfielder playing to the batter's slice side will play a shallower position. The two flank outfielders station themselves approximately midway between the two bases in front of them.

2. Strong Left Defensive Alignment (Diagram 4-2)

The coach signals this alignment by raising only the left arm as he looks out at his players from the dugout area. The players may also think of this signal as pulling strongly toward that foul line closest to the coach's

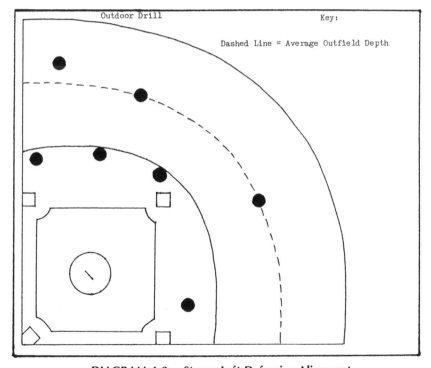

DIAGRAM 4-2: Strong Left Defensive Alignment
The third base line along with the entire left side of the diamond is well guarded at the expense of the right side of the diamond.

raised arm. Later, an opposite alignment will be signaled by raising the opposite arm. In this strong left alignment, the defense is preparing itself for what they feel is a strong right-handed pull hitter. For this reason, the defense will risk leaving most of the right side of the diamond poorly guarded in exchange for a strong concentration of players toward the left half of the field and the third base line in particular. It will usually be a strong right-handed number three, four, or five hitter that will command such a defense.

The left fielder plays four steps deeper than usual while the other two outfielders play at normal depths. He also moves to a pulled position located midway between his usual position and the left field foul line. In like manner, the center fielder moves to a position midway between his usual straightaway position and the usual straightaway position of the left fielder. That should place him in left-center field. The right fielder also moves to the midway point between his usual position and that of a straightaway center fielder, placing him in right-center field.

The third baseman plays both a deep and a strong pull position, guarding against a ball being hit down the third base line. The shortstop also plays deep and over to the third base side, covering what would normally be the hole between the third baseman and shortstop. The second baseman stations himself deep and almost right up the middle. Finally, the first baseman plays as far toward second as possible to help cover some of the area left unguarded by the second baseman. However, he can't allow himself to play so far over that he would be unable to return to the bag to take a throw from another infielder following a ground ball.

3. Strong Right Defensive Alignment (Diagram 4-3)

As might be expected, this defense is signaled by a raising of the coach's right arm. It is used to defense a strong left-handed hitter who would be thought to pull the ball in the direction of the right field foul line or, at least, to the right half of the field. The right fielder, playing four steps deeper than usual, positions himself at a point midway between his straightaway position and the right field foul line. The other two out-fielders play at their usual depth. The center fielder plays in right-center, midway between his own straightaway position and the straightaway position of the right fielder. The left fielder moves to left-center field, midway between his own straightaway position and that of the center fielder. The first baseman plays deep, guarding against the hard-hit ball down the line. The second baseman plays deep and toward first base, covering what normally would be the hole between the first and second baseman. The shortstop also plays deep and almost directly behind

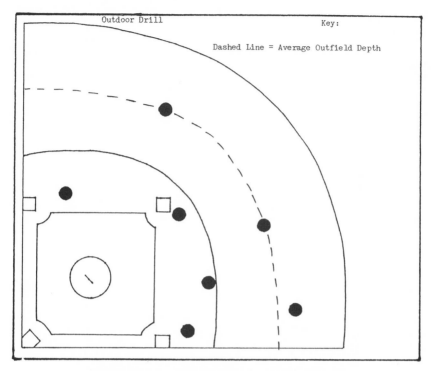

DIAGRAM 4-3:   Strong Right Defensive Alignment
As with the Strong Left Defensive Alignment, this alignment uses only two
players to cover half the entire field.

second base, giving himself a chance to cover a lot of ground including
much area on the right side of the infield. Finally, the third baseman plays
at average depth, but far off the third base line.

4. Slight Left Defensive Alignment
   (Diagram 4-4)

In this alignment, the defensive movements are in the same direction
as for the strong left alignment discussed earlier, but to a lesser degree.
The signal, too, is similar. The difference, though, is that while the coach
still raises his left arm high over his head, he directs his right arm and
hand to point to and touch the area opposite the elbow of the raised arm
(Photo 4-1). This alignment is called when some pulling of the ball is
anticipated, but perhaps to a lesser extent. Perhaps the hitter is not
exceptionally strong, but in past performances seems to be often out in
front of the ball, thus directing it more to the left side of the diamond. This

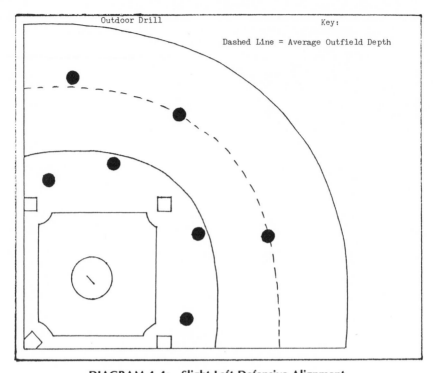

DIAGRAM 4-4: Slight Left Defensive Alignment
This alignment may very well defense a right-handed "lunge" type of hitter
who will often contact the ball weakly, but out in front of the plate, causing
the ball to be pulled slightly.

defense could also be directed against a left-handed hitter who hits a lot to
left field.

Because right-handed hitters get a better view of the pitch coming
out of the hand of a left-handed pitcher, they are more apt to pull against
such a pitcher. In this alignment, the left fielder plays slightly deeper than
normal (about two steps) while the center and right fielders play at their
normal depth. The amount of lateral movement by the outfielders is exactly
half of what it is for the strong left alignment. Therefore, the left fielder,
instead of moving halfway to the foul line from his straightaway position,
moves only a quarter of the distance. One method of easily determining
this distance is to first "eyeball" where the halfway point to the foul line
would be located and then to again eyeball half that distance and move to
that spot. Remember that half of one-half is one-quarter. Again, approx-
imations are just that...approximations. Only when defensive alignments

PHOTO 4-1: Arm Signal for a Slight Left Defensive Alignment
The use of the right arm and hand to touch the elbow area of the left arm differentiates this signal from that of the Strong Left Defensive Alignment.

become an exact science will precise distance determinations be expected and necessary. And that day will surely never come.

Using the same method, the center fielder moves one quarter of the distance between his straightaway position and what would be the straightaway position of the left fielder. In like manner, the right fielder moves toward center for a distance equal to one quarter of the distance between his normal straightaway position and the straightaway position of the center fielder.

In the infield, the third baseman still protects against a ball being hit down the line but does not play as deep since the hitter is not as likely to hit the ball as hard as someone being defended with a strong left alignment. The shortstop, while he doesn't move into the hole between short and third, does position himself deep and about two steps toward the hole. The second baseman plays fairly close to the base, but does not take as deep a position as required in the strong left alignment. The first baseman, however, continues to play as far to the second base side as possible as he does for the strong left alignment. This is also a good defense to use against a right-handed hitter who can hit to right-center, which should be adequately covered in this alignment by the right fielder.

5. Slight Right Defensive Alignment (Diagram 4-5)

The signal for this alignment is the opposite of that for the slight left alignment. The coach raises his right arm over his head and then touches his right arm at the elbow area. It is often used when a left-handed batter is being faced by a right-handed pitcher. With a strong left-handed pull hitter, a strong right alignment might be in order, but with the average left-handed batter, this alignment seems to serve the purpose. It can also be used against a late-swinging, right-handed batter who is apt to send the ball toward the opposite field. Against a left-handed hitter, the right fielder will play about two steps deeper than his normal position. The center and left fielders will play a normal depth. Bear in mind, though, that a late-swinging, right-handed batter calls for the right fielder to actually play a position shallower than his normal position by at least two steps, depending upon the size and strength of the hitter.

In this alignment, the right fielder moves a quarter of the distance to the foul line. Meanwhile, the center and left fielders move a quarter of the

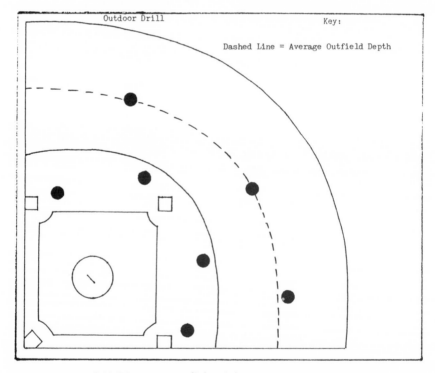

DIAGRAM 4-5: Slight Right Defensive Alignment
The third baseman, who must be watchful for a possible bunt his way, is the only infielder or outfielder who fails to shade to the right side.

distance between the straightaway positions of the outfielder toward which they are moving and themselves.

In the infield, the first baseman guards against the ball getting by between the foul line and himself. The second baseman moves about two steps in the direction of the hole between first and second and assumes a slightly deeper than normal positioning. Meanwhile, the shortstop plays at normal depth, but about two steps in the direction of second base. Finally, the third baseman probably will not see the ball hit toward him with this type of late-swinging, right-handed batter or left-handed pull hitter. Therefore, he would be best to play a straightaway position unless a bunt might be in order.

6. Middle Squeeze Defensive Alignment (Diagram 4-6)

The coach signals this defense by placing his hands together in "prayer fashion" and holding them over his head as does the football referee when signaling a safety. In this alignment the defense, expecting

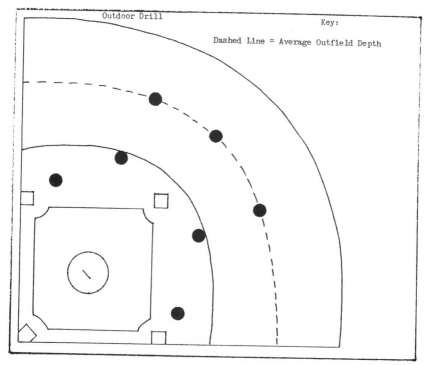

DIAGRAM 4-6: "Middle Squeeze" Defensive Alignment
Every infielder and outfielder shades toward the middle line of the diamond, thus giving up any defense of the foul lines.

the ball to be hit up the middle rather than pulled, leaves the foul lines unguarded in order to instead crowd the middle of the infield and outfield. With all the outfielders at their usual depth, the left fielder positions himself in left-center while the right fielder moves to right-center. The center fielder, of course, plays straightaway. The first and third basemen play in their straightaway positions, giving the batter the foul lines. Meanwhile, the shortstop and second baseman play in their straightaway positions, but deep to provide for greater lateral movement.

ADJUSTMENTS TO DEFENSIVE ALIGNMENTS

Adjustments may be in order with any of the six alignments for one reason or another. Infielders, for instance, will still be responsible for holding close to the bag any runners that may be on base. That could easily require some compromise to the suggested movements described. Outfielders must remember, too, that it will always be a little easier to track down a ball that's been hit to their glove side. Therefore, whether flanked by two outfielders or by one outfielder and one foul line, the advantage of moving after a fly ball hit to the glove side might well allow him to shade as much as a step away from this glove side.

DEFENSIVE ALIGNMENT FAILURE

Finally, with any kind of strategy there comes the chance of a backfire. That certainly will occur not once, but a number of times every game as the batters come up and respond to the defensive alignment constructed against them. Before becoming too discouraged at this prospect and perhaps entertaining thoughts of discarding this strategy, first investigate what might cause such a backfire. Knowing the causes may help reduce their numbers in the future. There are four possible reasons.

To better understand these reasons, consider, for example, a number three batter who in his first plate appearance lines a single to center field. Now, as he comes to bat for the second time, the coach calls for a straightaway defensive alignment. The batter responds with a fly ball pulled well to left field that falls uncaught near the foul line for two bases. The fly would probably have been caught had the defense been in a strong left or even a slight left pull. Instead, the maneuver backfired. What went wrong?

Reason #1—Misinformation. Major league teams use scouts and statisticians to chart the balls hit by every member of the opposition over a long period of time. That makes for a great advantage over a coach who watches an opponent for the first time and sees him single to center. Perhaps if this hitter could have been charted over his fifty previous appearances, it would have been found that he more often than not pulls the ball hard toward the third base side. Knowing that, the coach would surely have made the more appropriate choice of calling for a strong pull defensive alignment. In our example situation, the coach was forced to call a defense based on one plate appearance. This is understandably asking a lot. As a batter is seen more and more, everyone will gain a better idea regarding his geographic hitting tendencies. In this situation, the coach must also note the type of pitch, the count, and the position of the batter in the order as he singles to center. What if it was a number four hitter fighting to make contact with a curve over the outside corner while holding a count of 0–2? Even a strong, right-handed pull hitter will usually take a defensive attitude at the plate under these conditions and just try to make contact. The decision, then, to call for a particular alignment must be tempered by such variables, especially when only one or two plate appearances have been seen of a batter. That's why the taking of written notes or at least mental notes during the opposition's batting practice can pay big dividends.

Reason #2— Lack of Follow-Up Movement. Let's assume that a straightaway position was the correct, or at least the best, defensive alignment for the coach to call for the batter in our example situation. Now the outfielders must consider the many factors that they normally use to determine their positioning when a defensive alignment has not been called for them. Although the left fielder has been signaled to take a straightaway position at the outset of this batter's appearance at the plate, that does not mean he may not have a number of good reasons for beginning to shade a little or even a lot toward the third base foul line. Perhaps a crosswind is blowing in that direction. Perhaps this right-handed batter is being faced by a left-handed pitcher who doesn't throw very hard. Perhaps the outfielder has been relayed the fact that a curve ball has been called for on the upcoming pitch. Perhaps the count has moved to 3–0 as this normally defensive hitter gets the green light and begins to grow in confidence and aggressiveness as he awaits the next pitch. Yes, he may indeed be a straightaway hitter, *but not right now.* At this moment, a number of factors have converted him into a strong pull hitter, *at least for this one pitch.* Consequently, it becomes crucial for the outfielder to continuously weigh these factors in light of the original defensive alignment called by the coach and to move accordingly. He should remember that responding to the coach's call for one of six defensive alignments is only the "beginning" of his positioning for that batter.

Reason #3—Place-Hitting. Some batters are gifted with a better-than-average ability to place-hit the ball. Occasionally, then, when such a batter views the defense in a particular alignment, he will try to counteract it by "hitting it where they ain't," as the great place-hitter, Wee Willie Keeler, used to say. However, the good news here is that because such an action requires the batter to swing in a manner unnatural to his normal hitting style, most hitters will forego the attempt to place-hit successfully.

Probably the most famous defensive shift ever devised was the Ted Williams Shift, where both the infield and outfield maintained an exaggerated right field pull defensive alignment. Although an awful lot of the left side of the field was left unguarded every time Williams came to the plate, he nonetheless decided to continue doing what he did best... hit the ball hard to the right side.

Whenever the batter is known to be a good place-hitter, it is usually best to use a defense that will not leave any one area overly unguarded. Therefore, a straightaway alignment is usually best.

Reason #4—Percentages Catching Up.   Even if a coach has a chance to watch a batter over dozens of plate appearances and deems him to be a straightaway hitter, what does that mean? Surely, it doesn't mean that the batter hits up the middle 100 percent of the time. No one hits the ball into the same area 100 percent of the time or anywhere near that number. When he doesn't hit it there, the ball will usually travel to areas near that straightaway position, but will also, on occasion, be strongly pulled toward the third base line or sliced wickedly in the direction of the first base line. This is nothing more than a case of the percentages catching up with the defense. Sometimes, this "bad luck" is actually related closely to some of the facets discussed under Reason #2. If this is the case, then some of this misfortune can be avoided or at least minimized. However, most of the time, it is the result of dozens of inconceivable and incomprehensible factors that get blended together into this one swing of the bat that sends the ball flying or rolling in a direction that had not been counted on. Call it bad luck if you will or just consider it to be the percentages catching up with the defense that is trying to play according to a player's propensities. These occur in every game, though, so no apologies are in order.

Despite the backfires that will occur, utilization of these six defensive alignments remains a worthwhile strategy. They are, of course, only one tool that teams have in their arsenal for positioning stratagems. Like the many others discussed in this chapter, they will never become an exact science but will certainly bring about a greater number of successful outcomes than the use of pure chance. The outfielder who plants himself in the same place for each hitter is doing a great disservice to his team and himself. If the use of these defensive alignments proves successful even 51 percent of the time (and surely the number must be much higher, though incalculable), then their use must be considered worthwhile.

POSITIONING DICTATED BY GAME SITUATIONS

The six defensive alignments along with all the other factors upon which outfield positioning is determined are all based on commonsense logic and probability. Yet, there are a few instances when we must abandon these usually reliable guidelines and instead determine positioning by a closer look at the game situation.

Perhaps the most common such game situation occurs late in a close game with no one on base and usually two outs, but sometimes less. The coach will often move his outfielders a bit deeper to guard against the double, which would of course place a runner in scoring position. In addition, the left and right fielders would be shaded toward the foul lines for the same reason. This way, a hard base hit down a foul line could be handled fast enough by the outfielder to hold the runner at first. This is especially important when that runner represents the tying or winning run in a ball game. The first and third basemen would also shade to guard their respective foul lines.

Another situation that will occasionally present itself is the "slug-fest" game. Here, the pitchers just can't seem to get anyone out. Balls are rocketing all over the park, and because the pitchers are having a tough time, the hitters are throwing caution to the wind and are being very aggressive at the plate regardless of the count. To make the best of a tough situation, it would be best to play a lot deeper to cut down the number of extra base hits and hold some of them to nothing more than long singles.

Finally, with the winning run stationed on third in the last inning, a shallow-enough position should be taken from which to throw out the runner at the plate following a fly ball. This way, too, it might be possible to catch a line drive that would otherwise drop in for a hit. Obviously, it would serve no purpose to catch a fly ball in this situation at a depth from which the outfielder could not possibly throw out the runner. Of course, with two outs, no tag-up play is present, and thus, no such shallow positioning is necessary.

To communicate any of these adjustments to the outfielders, the coach merely gets their attention and then uses a two-handed pointing motion either laterally, out in front of him, or back toward himself.

MOVEMENT BY THE COUNT

Generally, the hitter can be expected to pull or hit with greater power as the count climbs in his favor. However, as the batter goes behind in the count, his aggressiveness diminishes because he just wants to make contact. Hitting defensively, then, causes this batter to wait longer and hit with less power, often toward the opposite field.

This phenomenon led to a number of studies comparing the batters' counts with their resulting actions. Such studies have suggested certain guidelines for the outfielders to follow for each and every count change. While far from an exact science, these suggested outfield movements do provide yet another tool through which to attain a more intelligent and probable fielding position.

To be effective, all three outfielders must shift as a group for a more balanced defense as opposed to leaving too big a hole in one area of the outfield. Obviously, a strike will always cause the outfielders to move away from the pull side while a ball call will move them toward that pull side. The center fielder moves left or right along a curved path, as would any point along the circumference of a circle. The left and right fielders, however, when moving toward a foul line, move diagonally at a 45-degree angle. This way, the flank outfielder playing on the pull side of the batter will not only be moving closer to the foul line as the count goes deep into

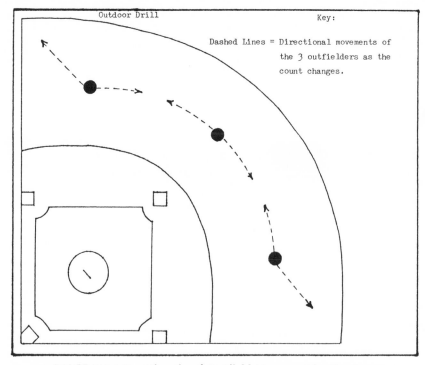

DIAGRAM 4-7:   Directional Outfield Movement by the Count
This strategy suggests any one of six possible outfield step movements for each of the sixteen possible changes in count.

the batter's favor, but will also be assuming a slightly deeper position with each ball call. Further, such a diagonal movement will keep him out of foul territory and out of a shallow position in the case of a 3–0 count (Diagram 4-7).

Below are indicated the 16 changes in count along with the corresponding suggested movements of the outfielders.

As the count changes from:

0–0 to 0–1,	move 2 steps to the	opposite field.
0–0 to 1–0	4	pull
1–0 to 2–0	4	pull
1–0 to 1–1	4	opposite
0–1 to 0–2	4	opposite
0–1 to 1–1	2	pull
2–0 to 3–0	4	pull
2–0 to 2–1	6	opposite
3–0 to 3–1	4	opposite
1–1 to 1–2	4	opposite
1–1 to 2–1	2	pull
2–1 to 3–1	6	pull
2–1 to 2–2	2	opposite
2–2 to 3–2	4	pull
1–2 to 2–2	4	pull
3–1 to 3–2	4	opposite
0–2 to 1–2	2	pull

Of course, neither these nor any other suggested count movements will ever guarantee success, but the logic behind them will surely provide good results more often than not. It is simply a way of playing the percentages. For best results, the other environmental and strategic positioning factors should continue to be used to determine positioning for the first pitch to each batter. As indicated in Diagram 4-7, the three outfielders must move as a unit to be effective and should move along the dashed lines.

BACKUP ROLES AND RESPONSIBILITIES

So far, all of the positioning discussed has been one of two varieties. The first dealt with positioning prior to the first pitch to a particular batter. Factors included the ballpark layout, wind, knowledge of the batter, and the many other guidelines mentioned in the discussion of defensive alignments. Then, after the first pitch to a batter, the outfielders' movements were determined by the changes in count.

Once the ball is hit, however, a third type of positioning comes into play. Unless the ball is hit to him, every outfielder has numerous backup roles and responsibilities. Outfielders usually do an adequate job in backing up their flank outfielder(s) to whom a ball is hit. What must be constantly worked on, however, are the many backup responsibilities on thrown balls. The outfielder should also consider "possible" follow-up throws in determining his best position. Since only a small percentage of these throws will make their way into the outfield, lazy outfielders will be slow to move into these positions. The aggressive outfielder, however, realizes the importance of these backup roles and pushes himself hard to be where he should be on every play. This facet of positioning requires a lot of self-discipline. Everyone talks about having an aggressive offense, but having a team of outfielders who are constantly backing up each other and moving in toward the infield for errant throws makes their defensive play truly aggressive. Following is an instructional breakdown of these backup responsibilities for each of the three outfield positions.

Left Fielder

1. On balls hit to center, back up the center fielder. Let him know if a runner is trying to tag up and advance as he is preparing to catch a fly ball. On all upcoming throws by the center fielder, call out "Perfect Throw" to remind him of the importance of that throw.

2. Move in toward second or third base quickly whenever the pitcher or catcher is seen beginning to make a pickoff throw toward that base.

3. Call out an alarm when a runner is seen beginning a steal of second or third base. If the pitch is not hit, quickly move into position to handle any errant throw.

4. Treat every ground ball to shortstop or third base as if it will go through into the outfield. Not only might the infielder commit an error, but he might also slow down the ball just enough to entice the runner to try for two bases on the play. In either case, charging in toward the ball is the proper play to make whether it ever gets through the infielder or not.

5. Move in to back up second base on throws to that base from either the first baseman, second baseman, or the pitcher, in the case of ground balls. In addition, back up the throw of the right fielder in toward second following a base hit to that field.

6. Move in quickly on any rundown that ensues between third and home, or between second and third. In both cases, move into the third base area for possible misplays, but also to possibly take part in any extended rundown in the absence of a third baseman.

7. Move in to back up third base on throws from the pitcher, catcher, first baseman, second baseman, or right fielder. In fact, third base must be backed up by the left fielder on any throw made there by any infielder, but also and especially the right fielder. Sometimes, with a runner on first, a bunt-and-run play may be attempted. Although the original throw may go to first base, a return throw will often be made to third base. Any overthrow there must be handled by the left fielder.

Center Fielder

1. Back up both the left and right fielders on all balls hit to them, whether fly balls or base hits. To be in perfect position to help out, move over as if anticipating an error. On a fly ball, let them know if a runner is tagging up. On any upcoming throw, call out "Perfect Throw" to emphasize the importance of hitting the relay man with a good throw.

2. Call out an alarm whenever a runner is seen stealing a base. With a steal of second, move in quickly to field any misthrown or misplayed ball to prevent any further advance by the runner.

3. Back up second base on pickoff attempts there by either the pitcher or catcher. While not wishing to tip off the play, the center fielder should, nevertheless, be informed by a signal from either an infielder or from the coach in the dugout. That way, he won't be taken by surprise as the pickoff begins to unfold. On the other hand, don't tip off the pickoff play by moving in toward second prematurely. Certainly, too, no movement toward the infield should be made on a pickoff attempt by the catcher until the pitch has passed the batter. Never try to place yourself on the receiving end of a pickoff attempt at second base by trying to sneak in behind the runner. With no one to back up the play, it is just too risky a play to incorporate into a team's play book.

4. On any rundown involving second base, move in quickly toward the bag to handle any possible overthrow coming that way as well as to possibly get involved in a prolonged rundown.

5. Back up second base on throws by the first baseman or any other infielder whenever a force-out or double play is attempted there.

6. Every ground ball to the second baseman or shortstop must be viewed as if it will either get through the infielder or be slowed down by him. Either way, then, move in toward the ball quickly to prevent the runner from advancing an extra base.

Right Fielder

1. Like your counterpart in left field, back up the center fielder on fly balls and hits to center field. Let him know when a runner is tagging up on a fly ball. On every upcoming throw by the center fielder, call out "Perfect Throw" to emphasize the importance of an accurately thrown ball to the relay man.

2. When a runner is seen attempting a steal of second base, call out an alarm and then move in toward the base in case a bad throw comes out in the direction of short-right field.

3. Move in toward second base whenever any throw is being made there by either the third baseman or shortstop in a force-out or double-play attempt. An overthrown ball would find itself traveling in the direction of right or right-center field.

4. Back up first base on all pickoff attempts there by the pitcher or catcher and also on any throw across the infield to throw out a runner at first. Also, quickly move in toward first on all bunts. While you may only rarely be able to prevent a runner from taking second on an errant throw, you can almost always prevent that runner from advancing to third, unless playing a pull position toward left field.

5. Help to cover first base in any rundown situation there. This is especially important when, with runners on first and third, the runner at first either walks off or is caught flat-footed with too much of a lead-off. Because the pitcher must back up the catcher, it is imperative that the right fielder get to first quickly to receive a possible second throw to that base in a rundown of the back runner.

6. Like the other outfielders, treat every ground ball hit to the right side of the diamond as if it will get through the infielders. If the ball gets through or even if it is just slowed up by an infielder, a charging right fielder should prevent the runner from taking an extra base.

In conclusion, a few reminders are in order for every outfielder regarding his backup role:

1. First, be well aware of any and all oral and verbal signals for pickoffs. However, be careful not to give away the play by any obvious pre-play movement or positioning in toward the infield.

2. Next, whenever backing up another outfielder on any kind of ball, let that outfielder know where to throw the ball if there are runners advancing on the play.

3. Third, upon seeing a runner break on a steal, never leave your position in anticipation of a backup role until the ball passes the batter. The play may actually be a hit-and-run play, which could see the ball being hit past the incoming outfielder. Even if a pitchout sign has been detected, remember that the ball could still be hit if it is pitched "wildly" over the plate.

4. Finally, in backing up a base, remember to remain far enough back to be able to react quickly enough to an errant throw. Being stationed less than about forty feet behind the infielder could easily result in the ball getting past you as well.

Commenting on the positioning and backup responsibilities of outfielders, former major league manager Gene Mauch once said, "I want my outfielders tired at the end of a game. If they aren't, they are not doing a good job!"

DRILLS AND METHODS OF INSTRUCTION

As in Chapter 3, the concepts of team positional play are best taught beginning in a chalktalk type of setting such as a classroom. Once the players have been introduced to the six team alignments and the strategy of "movement by the count," the drill setting can move outdoors. There, the outfielders can be drilled in all these movements with armylike drill commands mouthed by the critiquing coach.

Backup roles and responsibilities can be similarly taught culminating with the coach calling out situations to a complete defense. With the use of runners and with fungo in hand, the coach is able to drill every backup situation presented earlier.

Drills: Team Outfield Alignments

The six outfield defensive alignments are best taught in two parts. First, at the chalkboard, begin by fully explaining the mechanics of the movements, their signals, and the thought going into this strategy. Also explain the necessity for making certain strategic adjustments to these alignments at times. Finally, dispel any notion that these alignments are expected to be a Pandora's Box by detailing the four reasons why a particular alignment may backfire. Conclude with some positive statements of this very worthwhile strategic positioning tool.

The second part of this unit drill takes place on the field with every outfielder in place. If two or three outfielders are playing the same outfield position, they merely stand, in drill fashion, one behind the other but spaced several feet apart. Then, signal for one of the six defensive alignments and watch the response of the outfielders. Eventually, signal all the alignments, repeating them as often as necessary until the movements are fully understood by all. Answer any questions and, of course, critique along the way. Multi-positional outfielders must eventually get moved to their secondary outfield position to drill from there as well.

While the outfielders may be drilled separately out on the field, eventually both the infielders and outfielders must be drilled together to see how the entire team must shift as a defensive unit in response to any of these alignments.

Drills: Movement by the Count

Because the movement-by-the-count strategy bears so many similarities to the strategy of the six defensive alignments, its teaching and drilling may be handled similarly, using the same methodology as that just described.

Drills: Game-Dictated Positioning Adjustments, Backup Roles and Responsibilities

The handful of positioning adjustments necessitated by game conditions along with the many backup responsibilities of each outfielder can be handled together in a classroom setting. There, the importance of these movements can be emphasized after the strategy of the various count movements is explained. Then, out on the field, these movements and backup responsibilities are practiced by way of the familiar situation drills. With a full team on the field and utilizing runners for best results, the coach, with fungo in hand, calls out a situation. The situation then unfolds as the coach hits the ball, and the baserunners go into action. Then, the all-important response of the defense is observed and critiqued. Situations are repeated as necessary. For these situation drills, you will especially want to call out those situations that you feel demand a strong backup response by the outfielders. You may wish to provide yourself with a list of them as derived from the checklists provided earlier for each of the three outfield positions.

Positioning movements, whether performed to prepare for a batter or in response to a ball hit to another fielder, are physical acts, of course, and as physical acts go, require only the ability to walk or run a short distance. The problem, however, is that every outfielder realizes that 90 percent of the time, despite his perfect execution of these movements, the ball will not come his way. Most of the time, because the fielding has been flawless, the outfielder's backup positioning will not find him handling the ball. For that reason, to prepare for that one time in ten when the pitch will be hit his way or his help will be required in a backup capacity, the positioning and backup movements become an act that needs an abundance of patience and self-discipline. Yet, that's a trait found in the truly great outfielders and lacking in many of the others. It's no wonder that the great outfielder is seldom far from any ball that comes his way, and why he always seems to be "on the spot" when an errant throw eludes an infielder in front of him. It is the self-discipline and concentration that will present the greatest challenge to every outfielder when it comes to positioning. By comparison, the physical part, once committed to memory, becomes "a piece of cake."

____ Chapter 5 _____

Mastering the Fly Ball

INTRODUCTION

With his knowledge of positioning, the outfielder has now situated himself where he feels most ready to deal with whatever type of ball may come off the hitter's bat. One of the most exciting plays that may be put in action by the batter is the fly ball. It may require the outfielder to move laterally, move in, or move back. Its course may be affected by a strong wind, while its sighting may be limited by the sun's rays. It might be termed a "blast," "liner," or a "can of corn," depending upon its characteristics.

Regardless, it still remains the outfielder's job to track the ball down successfully before it falls in for a hit. Physicists debate theories to explain just how the human brain can determine where that ball is going to descend. The debate may continue, but meanwhile coaches and outfielders must work together with what knowledge exists to learn the most reliable and time-tested techniques leading to successful catches. That objective is the aim of this chapter.

THE STANCE

As a batter appears at the plate, the outfielder adjusts his positioning to the dictates of the coach, the infield captain, or the outfielder's own inclinations. Now, he assumes the stance he will use to await each pitch. Actually, there are three phases or movements involved with the stance.

Stance: The Resting Phase

The first of these three movements might be termed "the resting position." While there will always be some positioning to do before the first pitch to a batter and again following each pitch, there will still be some time to pass. With one or more runners on base, the outfielder must use part of that time to study the situation to determine the likely route of any upcoming throw. During this time, any erect but relaxed position will do. Some outfielders pound their glove a couple of times to deepen the pocket; others take a deep breath and stand relaxed with their glove curled up along their side (Photo 5-1). Whatever it takes, the outfielder should relax!

Stance: The Waiting Phase

Square Stance

As the pitcher begins to look in for his sign, it becomes time to take on the second movement of the stance. The outfielder has rested, but now must go into his "waiting position." Whenever stance is discussed, it is usually equated with this second phase. Here, all powers of concentration must become focused on the actions of the pitcher and batter. To do this, the outfielder assumes a waiting square stance (Photo 5-2). This places the body in the best possible position from which to move either right, left, in, or back.

PHOTO 5-1: Stance: The Resting Phase
The Resting Phase is the most informal and unstructured of the three parts of the outfielder's preparation period.

**PHOTO 5-2: Square Stance: The Waiting
Phase**
For readiness to move quickly in any
direction, the center of gravity is kept low
while the weight remains over the balls of
the feet.

The square stance finds both feet facing the batter and comfortably
spread. The feet are parallel, for the most part, although the toes may be
pointed out slightly. The weight is kept under the balls of the feet. A low
center of gravity is strongly encouraged.

The hands may or may not be together. If apart, they may be placed
on bent knees. However, any hands on knees must be removed before the
pitch. Otherwise, the weight of the shoulders and upper body pushing
against the knees will only make a quick start more difficult to initiate.

A somewhat crouched position, though, is still encouraged. This
way, the batter's swing plane and the outfielder's eye level will be about the
same. Getting such a good perspective on both the angle of the pitch and
the angle of the swing will allow the ball to be picked up the instant it
leaves the bat.

Drop-Step Stance

Some outfielders, in lieu of the traditional square stance, will opt for
the less common drop-step stance (Photo 5-3). Here, the feet and body
await the pitch while turned 90 degrees. The direction of the turn is to the
field representing the batter's strength. This direction, then, would be to

**PHOTO 5-3: Drop-Step Stance: The
Waiting Phase**
This is an alternate, but less popular, stance
taken in the waiting phase.

left field for right-handed batters and right field for left-handed batters.
Some outfielders favor this stance because they feel it will provide them
with a greater start for the ball on a long drive hit toward the side to which
they have drop-stepped. Since the outfielder is immediately ready to begin
his crossover steps for such a long drive, this thinking is correct.
Unfortunately, not every ball will be hit in that direction and when it's not,
the drop-step stance could prove slower, especially when lateral movement
is needed to the opposite side.

For instance, if the outfielder is in a drop-step stance toward left field
and the ball is instead hit behind him, the first step, of necessity, will be a
not-too-efficient left foot pivot step. From there, he'll be able to begin
longer crossover steps beginning with his right leg. So, while this stance
may facilitate movement toward the long drive in one direction, it will be a
detriment to the quick start in the other direction. Movement in toward
the infield works equally well with either stance. In assuming the position
for the drop-step stance, the toe of the dropped or back foot is placed even
with the heel of the other foot in addition to the body's 90-degree turn.

The outfielder must still be convinced, though, that the ball stands
the best chance of being hit exactly where he is situated. In this way, he is

utilizing both the strategic and environmental factors of positioning along with a comfortable stance in awaiting the pitch.

In deciding the best stance to adopt, the outfielder should give both methods a fair try. Then, and only then, will the outfielder be able to decide which of the two stances provides him with the best combination of comfort and good jump. Usually, the square stance gets the nod.

Stance: The Reaction Phase

At this point, then, with either the square stance or drop-step stance in place, it comes time to turn complete attention from the pitcher to the batter and the bat in his hands as the pitcher begins his windup. After all, it will be from somewhere in the strike zone that any hit ball will originate.

So far, the outfielder has gone through the first movement of resting between pitches and the second movement of waiting with concentration while eyeing the batter, his bat, and the strike zone area. This second movement takes place during all of the pitcher's windup or kick and delivery.

The third and final phase of the stance is the reaction movement (Photo 5-4). If being "off with the crack of the bat" is to have any validity in reality, the outfielder must quickly do something to get his body in motion in pursuit of the ball in whatever direction it may be hit. Of course, the difference between getting a good or a bad jump on a fly ball may only be a split second, but it's that very tiny time differential that will spell the difference between an easy catch, a running catch, or no catch at all. To gain that split-second jump on a ball, there are two practices common to outfielders who are considered quick.

First, the outfielder must keep the weight off his heels. Otherwise, he will find himself hopelessly trying to affect a quick reaction to a hit ball from a flat-footed position. To keep that weight forward requires a forward movement of a short one or two steps. Hitters are taught to develop rhythm in their batting style with some pre-swing movement, often called a waggle. Infielders are also constantly keeping their legs moving in their down position while awaiting a pitch. Outfielders must do the same. It's easier to move quickly in a given direction when the body is already moving as the pitch is almost to the hitter. As any physicist would remind us, "A body in motion tends to remain in motion."

Second, what makes the outfielder appear even quicker, however, is his seemingly uncanny knack of producing this pre-swing movement in the direction the ball has been hit almost simultaneously with the actual

PHOTO 5-4: Stance: The Reaction Phase
The key to reacting at the crack of the bat is a concentrated reading of the batter's hips along with the location of the pitch.

contact. Success here comes by fixing the eyes, not just on the strike zone area but on the batter's swing as well. From this position, a great jump is very likely. By zeroing in on the swing of the batter, the outfielder is actually reading and reacting to the ball before it leaves the strike zone. It gives him some prior knowledge of the general direction the ball will probably take.

Sometimes the batter may be seen "turning" very well on the ball, thus tipping off a probable pulled shot. At other times, he may be detected going with the pitch to the opposite field or finding himself way out in front as a result of a lunging type of swing. These kinds of tip-offs along with some form of pre-swing movement and the use of the many positioning factors discussed in the last chapter will place the outfielder within reach of almost every ball hit his way.

With an outfielder combining the necessary components of resting, waiting, and reacting into the makeup of his stance, he is ready to begin thinking about the various types of balls that he'll be called upon to field. Confined to this chapter and the next are the techniques and intricacies of catching the many types of fly balls, beginning with what is always hoped to be the "routine" fly.

STARTING AFTER A FLY BALL

From the time a fly ball leaves the bat to the time it enters the outfielder's glove, about four to six seconds will elapse. In that time, the outfielder must accomplish three things. First, he must begin his break in the ball's direction. Second, he must communicate his intentions to make the catch to his teammates nearby. Third, he must position his body for the catch and, of course, make a successful catch. Despite its importance, the art of communication, which is second in this sequence of events, is discussed later, as are the special techniques for using sunglasses.

The Break to the Ball

Unless a drop-step stance is being used, the break to the left or right begins with a relatively short crossover step (Photo Series 5-5 and 5-6). A longer step inhibits acceleration. Breaking in any direction should be done at full speed except for the line drive hit directly at the outfielder. Slowing down is always easier than speeding up. Failure to break at full speed represents a loss of time and distance that cannot be made up. Furthermore, the additional time gained allows the outfielder a bit more time to better position himself and settle in for the catch.

While some long drives may appear to be out of reach, the outfielder never gives up. There is always a chance that the wind or the curving effect of the ball will produce unexpected results, thus allowing for a possible catch.

In his sprint to the ball, the outfielder can keep the appearance of the ball flutterless by running on the balls of his feet. Running flat-footed only jostles the spinal area, giving the ball a blurred and fluttery appearance. It's like trying to catch a towering knuckleball. Obviously, this only reduces the chances of making the catch. The balls of the feet, however, help greatly by working like the shock absorbers of a car.

In a long run for the ball, the actual reach should not occur until the last possible second. More ground can be covered if both arms are close to the body than if one is in an extended position during the chase. In keeping the arms in, he will produce a greater pumping action with each stride.

Positioning for and Making the Catch

The break to the ball is followed by communication techniques to signal intentions to make the catch. As mentioned, these are discussed later so as not to interrupt our look at the outfielder's entire sequence of body movements involved in his eventual catch.

PHOTO SERIES 5-5: The Outfielder's Break to His Right
Every lateral break begins with a short crossover step. Often this step is actually begun as part of the reaction-phase movement.

(a)   (b)

PHOTO SERIES 5-6: The Outfielder's Break to His Left
An all-out break in either direction is crucial since the time saved in this initial acceleration cannot be made up.

(a)   (b)

Following the initial break to the ball, then, comes positioning for the catch. When a running catch is necessary, ideal positioning will not be possible. With loftier fly balls, however, there will be time to get into the best possible position for both a sure catch and, if necessary, a follow-up throw. Such positioning involves two parts.

First, when approaching the ball, the outfielder must get his body under control by shortening his steps. That is, he must reduce the length of his strides so he can establish a solid foundation for the catch and be able to throw on the next step.

Second, positioning ideally occurs where the ball is descending as opposed to the outfielder arriving there at the last second. To accomplish this, he must "round off" the fly ball in order to catch it in front of him instead of off to the side. This will require the last several steps to be run along a path describing an arc, thus the term "rounding the ball." The belly button will then be pointed toward home plate, and with the outfielder positioned perfectly for the catch (Photo Series 5-7).

If a runner will be trying to advance after the catch, not only must the outfielder shorten his steps and round off the ball, but he must also stay back two strides from the spot where the ball is descending. Then he moves in to meet the ball to produce the necessary body momentum to get off a throw with something on it (Photo Series 5-8). The ball should definitely not be caught with "dead feet."

With or without runners on base, there are still several guidelines the outfielder should follow to ensure a good catch as well as good positioning for any upcoming throw.

First, to get the best possible view of the ball entering his glove, he should make the catch at eye level or above. When the ball contacts the glove at any lower position, no room is left for any adjustment or quick hand movement if the ball begins to pop out (Photo 5-9).

Second, a brief "give" of the hands should take place upon contact of the ball and glove to better cradle the ball and reduce its chance of popping out. Just like infielders, outfielders, too, must demonstrate "soft hands."

Third, the ball should be caught by the right-handed outfielder with his left foot forward to produce a quick and efficient crowhop for any follow-up throw.

To assure a good catch, it really makes no difference whether the ball is caught to the outfielder's left or right side or directly in front of him. However, it will affect the strength and accuracy of any upcoming throw. Catching the ball far to the glove side leads to difficulties, because it causes the arm to travel too far across the body before finally getting rid of the ball. This disrupts the rhythm and timing of the throw (Photo 5-10). Also, catching the ball too far to the throwing side carries with it some

PHOTO SERIES 5-7: Rounding the Ball to the Outfielder's Right

Lofty fly balls requiring lateral movement should be approached while running an arc path so the outfielder is facing home plate when the ball is caught.

(a)

(b)

(c)

PHOTO SERIES 5-8: Staying Back in Tag-Up Situations
Needed momentum for a follow-up throw can be generated by rounding
the ball as needed. The outfielder remains back a step or two to keep the
body in motion and then moves forward as the catch is made.

(a)

(b)

(c)

PHOTO 5-9: The Above-Eye-Level, Two-Handed Catch

Whenever possible, both of these criteria should be incorporated into the catch of a fly ball.

PHOTO 5-10: Catching the Ball Far to the Glove Side

This extreme upsets the timing of the arm and leg movements necessary for a strong and accurate throw.

problems, since the end result is an unnatural body turn lacking much leverage. This, in turn, usually produces a short-arm release due to the throwing hand being prematurely thrust into a short-arm position to keep up with the crowhopping feet (Photo 5-11). Therefore, the outfielder should search for a happy medium that will produce the best results. That medium may range from just a little left of the center line of the body to just a little right of that line. While most outfielders tend toward the latter, catching the ball just a little to the glove-hand side is actually more natural. Further, it provides the arm with time for a complete range of motion arm swing during the crowhop without being too slow (Photo 5-12).

Experimentation in practice is the key. Making catches at various locations to the left and right of the body's center line followed by throws will allow the outfielder to make his own determination of the best point of contact.

Finally, two hands should be used whenever possible despite the many unnecessary one-handed grabs that go on in the big leagues. The two-handed catch brings about three worthwhile results. First, it helps to secure the ball by allowing the bare hand to close the glove upon the ball's impact. Second, it provides more time to secure a good across-the-seams grip. Third, it allows for a quicker release of any upcoming throw.

PHOTO 5-11: Catching the Ball Far to the Throwing-Arm Side
A short-armed throw often results from this extreme catching position.

**PHOTO 5-12: Catching the Ball Slightly
to the Glove-Hand Side
of the Body**
This position usually provides for the most
efficient crowhop for most outfielders.
Through experimentation, however, each
outfielder must determine what works
best for him.

Communication

The catch of a fly ball begins with a good break and finishes with
good body positioning. However, sandwiched between these two vital
components is actually the second of the three actions that contribute to
the perfect catch...communication. Every outfielder must learn to effectively communicate his intentions to the teammates around him, both in
the outfield and in the infield. Everyone wants to make the catch, but for
whom will the attempt be easier, and who, if anyone, has priority in
trying for the ball? Lack of good communication skills will often result in
the ball needlessly dropping in rather than being caught. Three different
scenarios can lead to this result.

1. Sometimes neither of the two closest players to a fly ball will call
   for it, each thinking that the other will make the catch.

2. A second scenario occurs when the two closest players both call for
   the ball and then, because of faulty communication, both back off
   at the last second, each thinking that the other will be going
   through with his intent to make the catch.

3. Probably the most unfortunate recurring situation results when two players both call for the fly ball and attempt to catch it, even after hearing the other continue to call for it. So often, because neither will back off of his original call, a collision results. This not only causes the ball to be jarred loose and fall in but sometimes results in injury, too.

When proper communication skills are by-passed, the ball is still sometimes caught. However, the catch is made far more difficult when incorrectly called for by the player in poorest position. This can also result in the ball being dropped or dropping untouched to the ground. Even if the ball is caught, any follow-up throw would most likely prove unsuccessful due to the player's poor fielding position in making the catch.

Outfield communication is easy as long as the coach takes the time during the pre-season period to set down the guidelines and procedures he wants followed for every fly ball. Those guidelines and procedures need not be identical to the ones listed here, but they must, nonetheless, be thoroughly understood by all players. Only then can success be anticipated.

To begin, the call for a fly ball will usually come within the first three strides toward the ball. Loudly and clearly, the fielder pursuing the ball should call out, "I've got it!" not once, but several times until the ball actually enters his glove. A single call or even two may not be enough to keep the nearest fielder from trying to make the catch. The calls must be forceful and leave no doubt in anyone's mind who is taking charge of this fly ball.

With a strong wind blowing, care is needed to avoid a premature call for a fly ball that could be better handled by another fielder. Such a wind can easily push a fly ball headed toward one outfielder into the range of another.

Besides calling out "I've got it" several times, the fielder making the call needs the assurance of the fielder closest to him. This is key! This closest fielder must continue to assure the fielder who has called for the ball that the ball is, indeed, all his. This assurance must continue until the catch is made. Appropriate words might include, "You've got it! It's all yours! You've got it! Nobody near you!" This assures the fielder making the catch that no one is about to plow into him.

Only the two (or occasionally, three) ball-chasers should communicate. Never should any other player try to help by calling for one player or another to make the catch. This only leads to chaos and often a dropped ball as well.

Because the center fielder is usually the fastest, most aggressive, and surest glove of the three outfielders, he is given priority on fly balls to left-center and right-center that he can handle with reasonable ease. Good judgment, though, should always prevail in tag-up situations and plays where runners are advancing. The stronger-armed outfielder should make the catch in these situations if possible unless he would have to make that catch in poor throwing position. This could be caused by a long run for the ball.

Therefore, when two outfielders simultaneously call for a fly ball hit between them, the non-center fielder must back off his call. To do this, he quickly begins reassuring the center fielder that the ball is the latter's all the way. Meanwhile, the center fielder continues to call for the ball to leave no doubt that he intends to make the catch. Even with this kind of communication, though, the two converging outfielders will be very close to the ball and to each other before they determine between them just who will be making the catch. Therefore, to help avoid collisions, the center fielder attempts to catch the ball head high while the flank outfielder zeros in on a shoulder-high catch. Mechanically, the center fielder takes the inside route on all pulled balls and the outside route on all balls hit toward the opposite field.

On the short pop flies hit between the infielders and outfielders, the closest infielder should call for the ball if he feels he can get to it, even though he may have to make the catch with his back to the infield. However, if both the outfielder and infielder call for the ball simultaneously, the outfielder continues to call for the ball, while the infielder quickly backs off his call and begins reassuring the outfielder that the ball belongs to the latter. When the infielder understands that such short flies belong to him until an outfielder calls him off, he will gain that needed confidence to go after this difficult over-the-shoulder catch without fear of a collision.

When an infielder makes the first call on a short fly or deep popup, the outfielder should call the infielder off the ball only if (1) he can get to the ball with reasonable ease and (2) he feels that the catch by the infielder would be a difficult one. A difficult catch for the infielder is usually considered to be one requiring the catch to be made with the infielder's back to the infield.

Still another reason to call an infielder off of a difficult pop fly would be to be in better position to make a follow-up throw. For sure, an outfielder coming in for a short fly is in better throwing position than the infielder going out to attempt an over-the-shoulder catch.

If the outfielder knows that there is no way for him to get to the short fly, he continues to move in toward the ball, being ready to reassure the infielder in case the latter makes a call for the ball. If neither is able to make the catch, the outfielder will at least want to be able to pounce on the ball quickly after it falls in for a hit.

With these kinds of guidelines spelled out to the team, a few fly balls may still be occasionally dropped, but surely not because of poor communication between the fielders.

DRILLS AND METHODS OF INSTRUCTION

When coaches mention fly ball practice, thoughts of tracking down lazy, lofty, drifting fly balls quickly brighten the eyes and spirits of the outfielders. Catching those high fungo shots, especially in good weather, isn't much work. Instead, such flies have become lots of fun since those Little League days when they were much more of a challenge. Because few balls will fall to the ground, outfielders are confident and enjoy this limited challenge of a drill. But coaches can't be content seeing these balls caught if proper techniques are not used consistently. Sooner or later, use of poor techniques will catch up with the careless outfielder. Practice, then, must include work on every type of catch beginning with the stance and continuing through the catch itself. This also includes the communication between the two closest players. Further, never hesitate to practice and drill these techniques under such adverse conditions as gusty winds or a bright sun. Instead, these become ideal conditions under which to improve these skills most quickly.

Despite space limitations, pre-season indoor practices must not be devoid of drills for the outfielders. In fact, teaching proper stance with its sequential three-part movement can best start indoors. The gym provides a perfect setting in which the outfielders can be lined up in platoonlike fashion and drilled in the three-part stance movements of resting, waiting, and reacting. The players can be taken through one movement at a time, being told the importance and technique of each and scrutinized along the way.

Next, concentrate on drilling the start for a fly ball. The players would like nothing better than seeing the proper break technique taught in conjunction with fly balls of all sorts being hit to them outdoors. Unfortunately, what usually happens is that the actual catching of the ball takes up the total concentration of the outfielder. His break will usually be taken with little or no thought to its mechanics, right or wrong, or to its improvement. For that reason, the gym again becomes the perfect setting to drill footwork. You may drill as a group while arranged platoonlike or one at a time. Either way, call out directional commands with the players responding with a six-step, quick-reaction break in that direction. The player simulates the catch on the sixth step and then freezes in that location, positioning himself again for the next directional command. The commands should include: "In," "Lateral left," "Lateral right," "Left angle back," "Right angle back," "Deep left," and "Deep right." If working with one outfielder at a time, you may wish to eventually toss a ball as the various directional commands are called.

On the long, overhead drive, especially when a change of direction is required, no one asks much more than for the outfielder to catch up with the ball and make the catch. But with the easier fly balls, more time is available. The outfielder should be expected to use every device and technique he has learned to not only make the catch, but to make it with correct body and hand positions, whether a follow-up throw is upcoming or not. These techniques are best explained indoors where player movements can be closely scrutinized. Watch each player move his body to the ball, round it, and get the hands and feet into their most advantageous positions for the catch. Because fly balls of any consequence can't be hit or even tossed very far or high indoors, the drilling of the judgment involved in the catching of fly balls must be saved for the outdoors. As mentioned at the outset, catching fly balls off the coach's fungo bat is one drill that players love. Because outfielders can usually make the catches despite some bad habits, it often takes a lot to convince players of the importance of self-discipline in the use of these techniques with every applicable fly ball.

Outdoor batting practice is an often-overlooked opportunity for outfielders to work on their fly ball skills. To really benefit defensively, though, only three outfielders should be allowed to take up positions while batting practice is taking place. Allowing clusters of players, many often non-outfielders, to station themselves in the outfield during batting practice and fight over the fly balls doesn't do any good and should never be tolerated.

If practice going back on a ball is needed, the outfielders can be intentionally set up shallow.

To practice coming in for short fly balls, the outfielders merely position themselves deep. Batting practice is one time you shouldn't mind your outfielders playing out of position. What is important is that this valuable opportunity to practice outfield skills, especially the fly ball, not be wasted. This way, the outfielders will soon be wanting to be chosen as one of the three outfielders to be stationed there during batting practice.

Because rounding a fly ball and positioning for a catch is such an important skill, a couple of drills for that purpose are included here.

The first drill has all the outfielders positioned in either straightaway left or right field. A complete infield is also used. Take up a position near home plate and alternately fungo fly balls down the first and third base lines. This will require the left fielders to move to their right in rounding the ball while the right fielders will round the balls to their left. All the positioning techniques are given added importance when you direct follow-up throws to be made to second base, third base, or home. Of course, the third baseman is the cut man on throws to the plate by the left fielders, while the first baseman does likewise for the throws home by the right fielders. This drill keeps everyone hopping, especially since the cut man may cut a throw to the plate and redirect it to one of the other bases (Diagram 5-1).

If you would rather not get your outfielders involved with the techniques of follow-up throws, then you can resort to another drill that stresses the rounding concept, communication, and positioning skills, but little emphasis on throwing. This drill places all the outfielders in one of two lines in two adjacent outfield positions, such as left field and center field. No infielders are needed other than one player stationed about 120 feet away from the outfielders. He receives the throws and relays them to the player catching for the fungo-hitting coach, who is stationed to the side of the mound. Although all fly balls are directed midway between the

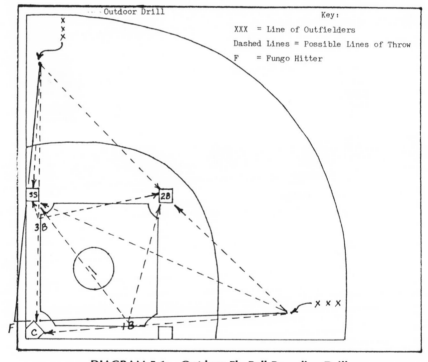

DIAGRAM 5-1:   Outdoor Fly Ball Rounding Drill
Although outfielders may be directed to throw to second or third base as well, this diagram shows the placement of infielders when a throw is made to the plate. The hitter alternates between the two baselines and allows the play to be completed before the next ball is hit.

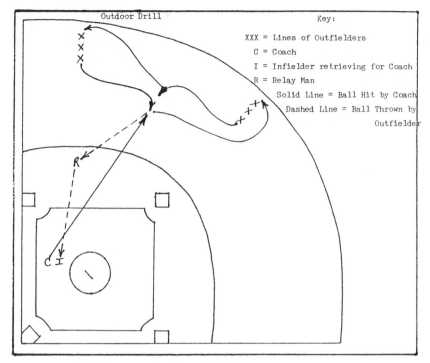

DIAGRAM 5-2:   Outdoor Fly Ball Rounding, Communication, and Backup Drill

Here, the left fielder makes the catch while the center fielder backs up the play. The relay infielder always aligns himself with a base just for the practice, even though no throw is made to a base.

outfielders, the two adjacent outfielders whose turn it is (one from each line) converge on the ball. The left fielder calls for the ball, rounds it, and makes the catch while communicating with the other outfielder who assumes a backup position. The two players then go to the ends of the opposite lines to gain practice both ways. Halfway through the drill, the coach reverses the drill, directing the center fielder to call for and make the catch while the left fielder communicates and backs up the play. This way, the outfielders will get practice in moving in both directions (Diagram 5-2).

Because wind conditions can create havoc with any fly ball, it is important to incorporate one or more of these fly ball drills whenever strong and gusty winds are present on practice days. Learning to break, communicate, and position for the catch under such conditions will better prepare players for similar game conditions.

Unfortunately, outfield communication is often thought of as something to be discussed at a team meeting, but that's all. It is a mental discipline, though, that must carry to the practice field as well. Insist that proper communication techniques be used for any of these drills for which there might be any doubt over who would be making the catch. This includes not only the call for the ball, but also the assurance response by the nearest backup outfielder.

More difficult than practicing communication among outfielders is the practice of infielder-outfielder communication required on those difficult short fly/deep popup variety of fly balls. For best results, a complete infield and outfield should be placed on the field. The outfielders should be positioned very deep while the infielders should be placed no more than medium depth. This way, both the infielders and outfielders will have to go a long way to catch up with a fly ball or a deep popup hit between them. For anyone to successfully make this catch off of a coach's fungo bat, a lot of communication will be necessary.

A tremendous aid to placing these flies about midway between the infielders and outfielders is the use of an adaptable pitching machine that can be made to propel the pitches upward. Slight adjustments can then be made to vary the depth of the fly balls and popups. Otherwise, the coach must rely solely on his accuracy skills with a fungo bat.

Chapter 6

Success With the Specialty Catches

INTRODUCTION

It would be so easy if every fly ball that made its way to an outfielder was of the lazy, routine variety hardly requiring any movement. Reality tells us, though, that some catches will call for exceptional play, often including a long run.

Unfortunately, there will be times when the outfielder's well-thought-out positioning plans will backfire. Instead, he will find himself far from the play and faced with a long run to the outer reaches of the outfield. Worse still, the long drive may appear to be taking a directly overhead route. Lost will be the luxury of rounding off the ball. Lost will be the well-planned, methodical movement forward for the easy, two-handed catch. Instead, in a split second, he will be forced to call upon every technique he has ever been taught to successfully handle this type of drive.

Perhaps the fly ball is a line drive hit directly in his direction. Will this drive sail over his head? Will it instead want to die and drop in front of him? Or perhaps he is in perfect position for the catch, but at the moment isn't sure of this fact as the line drive leaves the bat. What does he do in these situations?

When that line drive shot is seen to be dying quickly or when a fly ball requires a long, lateral sprint to the ball, an attempt at a diving catch may be necessary. Getting the glove under the ball before it's down is the first problem; making the ball stay in the glove is perhaps even tougher.

Another difficult catch is the ball that sends the outfielder back to the fence or close to it. Running into a wall or fence doesn't leave the body feeling too well. Consequently, there could be a legitimate hesitancy as the outfielder approaches the far reaches of the ballpark. Yet, because such towering drives come with the territory, he must use certain techniques along with any existing warning track to bring down a greater percentage of these long balls.

Finally, even with the most routine of fly balls, problems can occur when the ball is hit into the sun. In these situations, the outfielder must be well versed in techniques to battle the sun if the ball is to remain in sight for the catch.

Let's look at each of these plays in closer detail to determine the necessary steps to take, no pun intended, to effectively deal with them.

THE LONG DRIVE

One of the more difficult fly balls to contend with is the one hit long and *almost* directly overhead. The chase begins with a drop-step to the side to which the ball has been hit. This short backward step quickly readies the body for the crossover step sprint to the ball.

For instance, on a ball hit long, but to the right side, the drop-step is taken with the right foot. Now in a crossover position, the outfielder is in perfect position to begin the actual sprint to the ball (Photo Series 6-1). The drop-step to the outfielder's left side is shown in Photo Series 6-2.

A common mistake is to forego the drop-step and instead begin immediately with a crossover step to the ball side. This incorrect technique only produces a longer route to the ball. In addition, it will often

PHOTO SERIES 6-1: The Long Drive to the Outfielder's Right Side
The first movement is a drop-step made by the right foot followed by the necessary number of crossover steps to get to the ball.

(a)   (b)

Photo Series 6-1 (cont'd)

(c)

PHOTO SERIES 6-2: The Long Drive to the Outfielder's Left Side

It is imperative that the drop-step precede any crossover steps so as to keep the eyes within sight of the ball. It will also produce a shorter route to the ball.

(a)

(b)

continued on next page

Photo Series 6-2 (cont'd)

(c)

cause the outfielder to lose sight of the ball and may needlessly turn him around as well.

THE DIRECTLY OVERHEAD DRIVE

The outfielder's nightmare is the long drive hit *directly* over his head. The first movement will be a drop-step, of course, but to what side? And will it really matter? Interestingly, most of these drives will be curving on their way out and will consequently finish on the outfielder's left or right side. Two reasons account for this curving action.

A ball will usually slice when hit to a batter's opposite field. When hit to a batter's strength field, the ball will have a hooking action as it is pulled. Both phenomena find the ball curving toward the foul line. Left and right fielders must remain aware of this and be prepared, therefore, to begin with a drop-step in the direction of the nearest foul pole. The longer the drive, the greater the curve.

Although the center fielder isn't as affected by such slicing or hooking movement of the ball, like all outfielders he is susceptible, nevertheless, to the force and direction of the day's wind. This is the second cause of the ball's curve on a long drive. Overestimating the wind's strength is the key here. By overanticipating the possible effects of the wind, the outfielder won't find himself running great distances trying to track down wind-blown drives. So once again, what may have started out as a long drive hit directly overhead will instead become a much easier catch than anticipated. Throughout the game, he should be mindful of the possible effects of the wind. Sometimes, however, due to a judgmental error or because the ball really has been hit directly overhead, the drop-step may be made to the wrong side; hence, the drop-step is made with the wrong foot. When that happens, the outfielder is faced with the prospect of losing sight of the ball. This leads to two options.

The first option is to pivot on the dropped foot back to the other side without losing sight of the ball. The dropped foot, of course, is the one on which the original dropped stop has been taken. In so doing, the drop-step in the proper direction has taken place, but belatedly on the outfielder's second step instead of his first. This way, the over-the-shoulder catch can be made without losing sight of the ball. This correction technique could even take place following one or two whole crossover steps in the wrong direction (Photo Series 6-3). Once the pivot to the other direction is made, however, the outfielder should go immediately into crossover steps and not be tempted to backpedal. Backpedaling, which is nothing more than running backward, is the slowest way to track down overhead drives and often results in failure.

Unless a wind dictates otherwise, the center fielder will usually drop-step with the foot on his glove side. Hopefully, it will produce a catch that will allow him to follow the ball all the way into his glove as opposed to the slightly tougher backhanded catch.

While watching the ball all the way certainly has its advantages, a second method of handling the directly overhead drive advocates just the opposite. Upon realizing that sight of the ball is about to be lost due to a drop-step in the wrong direction, the outfielder immediately turns his back on the drive. He completes the turn while simultaneously sprinting to the spot where he hopes to find the ball descending. Then he resumes looking skyward to relocate the ball. This method, often used by the veteran outfielder, has the advantage of a more efficient and faster turning movement. Its disadvantage of intentionally losing sight of the ball for hopefully no more than a quick second is a big one. As a result, its use is advocated only after a lot of practice (Photo Series 6-4).

THE LINE DRIVE

One of the most difficult, yet least coached, types of fly ball is the line drive shot. Because line drives are hit sharply "on a line," they hang up for a much shorter amount of time than the lofty fly ball. Additionally, line drives hit to a batter's opposite field will slice toward the foul line as well

PHOTO SERIES 6-3: The Directly Overhead Drive - The Belated Pivot Method
Here the outfielder follows his drop-step with one crossover before executing the necessary pivot to the other side to prevent losing sight of the ball.

(a)   (b)

(c)   (d)

Photo Series 6-3 (cont'd)

(e)

(f)

(g)

(h)

PHOTO SERIES 6-4: The Directly Overhead Drive - The Complete Turn Method

In lieu of pivoting to retain sight of the ball, the outfielder completely turns his back to the ball while racing to that spot where he feels the ball will be descending.

(a)

(b)

(c)

(d)

Photo Series 6-4 (cont'd)

(e)   (f)

as the liner pulled to a batter's strength field. Left and right fielders must anticipate this slicing or hooking effect of the ball. Line drives hit to center field will usually lack this kind of lateral movement but, like liners hit anywhere, may just as easily sink as sail. When the liner is hit to the outfielder's left or right, he gets a better look at the spin and action of the ball. However, it's when the ball is hit directly at him that the play becomes one of the most difficult with which to deal.

In this situation where doubt exists about charging in or moving back, and without the luxury of a lot of time, the outfielder should refrain from charging at all cost. A charge is made only when no doubt exists that the ball is descending in front of him. The key to handling the line drive hit directly at him is to vie for time to determine the ball's force and hence, trajectory. To accomplish this, he waits for a split second while simultaneously pivoting to a drop-step position, if not already in one. Now, he will be in a better position to either charge or go back on the ball (Photo Series 6-5).

In attempting the catch of a sinking liner, the outfielder gets into a semi-crouch while running to lower his eye-view of the ball. With this better view, he waits until the last possible second before extending the glove. Running with an extended glove does nothing but slow down the fielder.

PHOTO SERIES 6-5: Awaiting the Line Drive Catch

The outfielder's key to correctly judging the strength of the line drive hit directly at him is to wait for a split second while assuming a drop-step position to become better prepared to move in or back.

(a)   (b)

   While catching fly balls with the fingers of the glove up is most natural, such a glove position for the line drive is possible only with easier liners that can be caught at waist level or above. Liners contacted below the waist must be caught with the glove fingers in a down position.

   The fielder should look the ball into the glove and use both hands whenever possible. A one-handed try, while less sure, does provide a greater arm extension as an overriding advantage. Either way, he tries to demonstrate soft hands in giving as the ball contacts the glove (Photo Series 6-6).

   On a liner that he decides to let drop in, the key is to get the body under control by shortening the steps and then getting the glove down like an infielder.

   If indecision finds him caught between a long and a short hop of a liner that has just fallen in front of him, the main priority must be to keep the ball in front of him and not let it get through. The body must be used to block and smother the ball any way possible.

   If the line drive is hit harder than first thought, the outfielder goes back on the ball from his now-assumed drop-step position as he would any fly ball hit directly overhead. These techniques have already been mentioned earlier in this chapter. Most important, though, he must remember

PHOTO SERIES 6-6: The Shoestring Catch

The glove is extended, only at the last second, from a semi-crouch position. The fingers of the glove are pointed down for any liner contacted below waist level.

(a)

(b)

(c)

to immediately assume the drop-step position whenever a line drive is seen coming directly at him.

When he determines that the ball is sinking fast in front of him, a second decision must be made. Does he attempt the shoestring catch or does he instead lay back and field the ball on a hop? On a long, lateral run for a ball, he must similarly decide whether to let the ball drop in and play the ball safely or go all out with a diving attempt. Following are some of the factors and strategies involved in that decision to dive or not to dive.

THE STRATEGIC DECISION TO DIVE

Learning to make the diving catch is one matter, but deciding when and when not to dive is quite another. The most overriding factor will be the outfielder's degree of confidence in being able to snare the ball before it hits the ground. Obviously, this involves a split-second decision. However, other determining factors exist and must be considered. Fortunately, they revolve around the field condition and game situation at the time. Every outfielder, if aware of these factors before the ball has even been hit, will be better able to make the right decision.

Whenever the outfield turf is soft, either from moisture or a well-manicured cushion of grass, the ball will not bound away too far if uncaught. He can be far more aggressive than on a dry, hard, or barren outfield, which will be very fast. When the diving attempt is unsuccessful, the ball could roll a long way.

Outfield geography is yet another factor. Dives for balls hit into the power alleys will always produce the luxury of a backup man nearby. That won't be the case, though, when the dive of a left or right fielder is made near a foul line.

With his team ahead in score by several runs, the outfielder can be more daring and aggressive with these kinds of balls. If he fails to make the catch, little is lost. However, a similar result occurring during a close game could be the catalyst to turning the whole game around.

Similarly, such attempts, for the most part, should not be made with two outs, unless the outfielder has a high degree of confidence in getting to the ball for the successful dive. By playing the ball on a hop and conceding the single, the offense, with only one out to go, must advance their runner three bases further to score. This will probably require two hits. The unsuccessful attempt will most likely leave the runner on second or third where only a single will be needed to score him.

Finally, if allowing the ball to drop in will allow a go-ahead or winning run to score in the last inning or late in the game, then the catch must be attempted.

THE DIVING CATCH

If a diving catch will be necessary, it's got to be all or nothing. Nothing short of an all-out effort will bring about a successful catch. While a one-handed catch will provide for greater extension, that arm is extended only as the dive is started and not before. Otherwise, the run for the ball will only be slowed.

To protect against the ball being jarred out of the glove upon contact, the elbow must be extended rather than bent. It is the impact of the bent elbow with the ground that so often causes the glove hand to open and send the ball dribbling out. To cushion that impact, the outfielder should semi-slide on either the chest or legs as contact is made with the ground, then use his hands to hoist himself back up quickly (Photo Series 6-7).

In diving for the short fly ball, a bent-leg slide is still another method of handling the diving catch. This way, the outfielder literally slides under the ball.

Sometimes, too, a left or right fielder may use this bent-leg slide technique after a running catch that finds him in foul territory quickly nearing a fence or wall.

THE CATCH AT THE FENCE

Like the diving catch, the catch of the long drive at the fence is another of those game-breaking plays. The catch may or may not require a leap, and it may or may not require contact with the fence or wall. However, if only because of the fence's proximity, it becomes a very special play, sometimes a game-breaker. There's bound to be some feeling of concern, if not downright fear. No one likes to run into such structures. Yet, because such plays come with the territory, the outfielder can't allow himself to be timid in going back on these long drives. Oftentimes, timidity coupled with inexperience may cause an outfielder to keep his eyes glued on the ball as he gently continues backward, all the while feeling for the fence. While he may still catch the ball, he certainly is hurting his chances. Such long, towering drives require instead that he momentarily take his eyes off the ball once its flight has been judged and run hard to the fence. At that point, he turns back to relocate the ball. It might be necessary to move back a couple of steps if the strength of the drive is overestimated or if the wind slowed it down.

Still more difficult is the long, line drive shot for which the outfielder will have even less time to locate the fence. Yet, even the briefest of glances will help, even though he may still be unable to get all the way back to it. It's not surprising, then, that so many of these long, line drive shots are

PHOTO SERIES 6-7: The Diving Catch

Keeping the glove arm straight upon making contact with the ground helps the outfielder keep the ball in the glove. Hitting the glove-side elbow into the turf often causes the glove to open and pop the ball loose.

(a)

(b)

(c)

caught with the outfielder in a less-than-well-balanced position. Of course, if the outfielder could get back to the fence easily on every drive, it would indicate that he was playing too deep.

With a low fence, a drive well over the outfielder's head will often go for a home run. A high fence or wall, however, may result in a carom of the ball back toward the infield. This is where awareness of the "bounce-ability" of this outfield structure is so useful. Of course, when the confidence is present, the leaping catch should be attempted. Otherwise, discretion should take over and the outfielder should back away from the fence or wall and face it squarely in anticipation of the carom. A concrete wall will produce a much harder carom than will a cyclone type of fence. The harder the rebound, the further from the fence or wall the outfielder should position himself to keep the ball from rebounding by him.

A warning track composed of either gravel, cinders, or sand is found on a number of fields. The track is used to help judge distance from the fence. Upon contacting it, the outfielder becomes better aware of his proximity to the fence. The mere difference in the feel of the footing will cause him to shorten or chop his strides in preparing to meet the fence or wall. It is key, though, to be aware of the track's distance from the fence. This way, he can often locate the fence without a collision.

Because so many fields have no such track, reliance must be placed on the outfielder's "feel" for the layout of the field. This is all part of positioning. He must have a feel for the distance from the fence each time he takes the field.

When the ball does send him back to where he believes the fence to be, he uses the nearest hand, whether gloved or bare, to feel for the fence or wall. He'll then know whether it's possible to go back any further. He should not make the play any tougher than necessary by failing to "give himself a hand" (Photo 6-8). Unfortunately, this tool cannot be used with line drive shots to the fence because of the time factor.

When an outfielder gets back to the fence and determines the fly to be within reach but definitely over his head, the makeup of the fence along with its height come into play. While a low fence cannot be climbed, the bare hand can be placed atop it to provide greater strength and leverage as the leap is made. For maximum leaping and for efficiency in making any follow-up throw, the outfielder should assume a sideways position as opposed to placing his back to the fence. A higher cyclone type of fence or vine-covered wall lends itself well for climbing. With his bare hand in or atop the fence or wall and his spikes catching hold for even a split second, the outfielder may be able to gain some much-welcomed height in his leap for the ball (Photo 6-9).

PHOTO 6-8: Feeling for the Fence
On long drives to the fence when time permits, the outfielder should feel for the fence with the nearest hand to determine the fence's proximity.

Finally, some long drives may be determined to be descending at the wall, but several feet to the left or right of the outfielder. In trying to gain added momentum for the leap, he should choose an indirect route to the ball. Locating the fence as close to himself as possible, he begins a momentum-building run alongside the fence, using his throwing hand to maintain a feel for the fence and to aid in his eventual leap. The

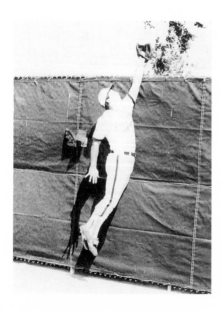

PHOTO 6-9: Leaping at the Fence
Unlike this heavy-tarp-covered fence, some fences are more easily climbed when ivy-covered or constructed of a cyclone type of fencing.

PHOTO 6-10: Shading the Sun With the Glove
Such shading, when produced at the correct angle, is often all that is necessary to make a catch in the sun.

inexperienced player would more likely move right to the point where the ball was descending. Such a successful leaping grab can do much to restore confidence to the pitcher who admittedly threw a bad pitch.

PLAYING THE SUN FIELD

Because the sun so often causes havoc to outfielders who must track fly balls through its harsh rays, techniques must be learned to cope with this environmental factor.

The most-often-used tool is the glove itself. With the sun low and a pitch on the way, the glove should be held up to the sun (Photo 6-10). Then, with the ball in the air, the outfielder should try sighting the ball preferably above, but sometimes below, the glove and make the catch. Looking directly into the sun is never suggested. If necessary, he should look for the ball at an angle away from the sun from which he feels the ball will emerge. When the sun affects his vision, he shifts his position slightly. This may result in being a few steps out of perfect fielding position. However, in tracking the ball into the glove, sighting it is far more important than being in perfect position but not seeing the ball. When a ball becomes lost in the sun, a new and better angle can be created by moving a few steps to the side. Often, the ball will reappear. This requires patience. Sometimes, the ball will even reappear without moving to a new angle. But if it doesn't, the outfielder should take some quick cover by turning away from the infield and bending while covering the head for protection.

Popular with baseball as well as football players are various eye blackener products. This is a shoe-polishlike material applied below each eye on the upper part of the cheekbone in about a two-inch strip. The ingredients of this sun-glare material help to deflect the sun's rays to some extent. With a fly ball in the air, the outfielder still shades the sun with his glove, but the use of eye blackener should facilitate the ball's tracking.

Finally, there are baseball sunglasses that contain flipdown lenses controlled with a tab on the side. The glasses are worn in the up position until needed. When the fly ball's line of flight is determined, the glasses are flipped down with a tap of the tab, making the spring-action lenses flip down (Photo Series 6-11). The glasses should never be flipped down until the ball is spotted, yet they should not be flipped down at the last second either.

Sunglasses should go on just as soon as it's determined that the sun might cause problems. It's very discouraging to watch an outfielder ask for

PHOTO SERIES 6-11: Using Outfield Sunglasses
The glasses should be worn with the lenses up until the trajectory of the fly ball is determined. Then the lenses should be flipped down immediately.

(a)   (b)

sunglasses after just having lost a fly ball in the sun. In fact, to really become proficient in their use, outfielders should wear sunglasses on sunny days in practice. Needless to say, every serious-minded outfielder should own his own pair. Remember that the glasses and strap should go on before the cap.

When a fly ball is in direct line with the sun's rays, even sunglasses may not be the complete answer. Here, the glove must complement the use of the glasses. The glove is held close to the face to provide more shade and steadiness. The fly ball in the sun is not a fun play, but it is one with which outfielders must learn to contend.

DRILLS AND METHODS OF INSTRUCTION

As the difficulty of the fly ball catch progresses from the routine to any of a number of tougher specialty catches, so too must the drills.

In one of the Chapter 5 indoor drills, outfielders were drilled to respond either one at a time or in platoonlike fashion to fly ball commands. As each command was called out, each outfielder responded with a six-step movement in the appropriate direction. Now, commands can be added for the "deep drive left," "deep drive right," and "overhead left" or "overhead right" balls. It would be wise, though, to first drill these separately before incorporating them with the other commands. Unless told otherwise, the outfielder will have a choice of two techniques to use in response to the "Overhead Left" and "Overhead Right" commands. On the command, the outfielder drop-steps to the commanded side and executes six crossover steps. He then uses one of the two recommended turns to the other side and then follows with another six steps when the make-believe catch is made. Only then should this drill be attempted outdoors with a thrown or machine-directed ball or a ball hit off of a fungo bat.

The most effective drill for the long overhead drive begins with the coach (with or without a ball-tossing machine) and the first of a line of outfielders standing at one end of the gym. The outfielder assumes his stance facing the nearest wall, but with the coach still in front of him. Upon command, he drop-steps toward the side directed by the coach. He then begins racing back with crossover steps while continuing to watch the coach or the machine. After the outfielder has taken about six steps, the ball is thrown by the coach or directed deep by the machine, but to the opposite side of the outfielder. This will require him to pivot in the direction of the ball without taking his eyes off of it. The more advanced technique will require the outfielder to completely turn his back on the ball while completing a 180-degree turn as he races to the point where he expects the ball to be descending. It will be when the ball is released by the coach or the machine that the choice between the two methods must be made. The coach may wish to work all the outfielders on one technique at a time. Later, he may allow them to choose the method with which they are more comfortable.

Still another drill used to teach this technique is the "One-Look Drill." It can be used indoors or outdoors. One at a time, each participating outfielder assumes a shallow position. As the outfielder drop-steps and begins his crossover steps in one direction, the coach throws, machine-directs, or fungoes a fly to the outfielder's opposite side. The player then uses the 180-degree turn technique to get to the ball. To run the drill as a game, outfielders must use this advanced technique of turning their back to the ball as they change direction. Because the trick is to be able to sprint to the point where the ball is expected to descend, the outfielder is allowed no more than three strides from the time he resumes his look upward for the ball to the moment he makes the catch.

Working on the catch of the line drive is best handled outdoors, of course, but the preliminary movement of making a drop-step pivot can be practiced indoors. When a liner is sinking quickly in front of a charging outfielder, a dive or shoestring catch may be necessary. While such conditions are difficult to reproduce outdoors using a fungo bat, they are, in fact, very easy to duplicate indoors using a thrown ball or a ball-throwing machine. With each outfielder, in turn, charging forward onto well-placed wrestling mats, the ball can be thrown (or directed by the machine) to descend at a point requiring a dive or shoestring catch (Diagram 6-1). Later when outdoors, having already been drilled in the dive and shoestring catch, the outfielders can be hit liners from a shallow position of about 200 feet. This way, there will be just as much chance that the outfielder will be forced to go back on the ball as charge forward. Either way, remind him to momentarily stall by pivoting to a drop-step stance while trying to get a better read on the ball. The outfielder will actually welcome the opportunity to go back on the rising liner. If the ball should carry over the head of the outfielder, the drill then focuses on the proper way to pick up a ball at the outfielder's feet. In time, the coach's hits will lengthen.

Practice will be in store for the coach, too, in his attempts to fungo liner after liner. While it may indeed present a challenge, the difficulty can be lessened if you remember the secret to hitting line drives. Think of the ball as being composed of five equally thick horizontal rings. Now, if you wish to hit a long, towering fly, you toss the ball up and contact it about chest-high along the third or middle ring. The greater the uppercut angle, the shorter but higher the fly. About a 45-degree angle swing is needed for maximum carry.

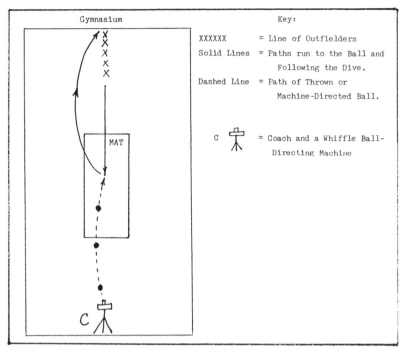

DIAGRAM 6-1:   Indoor Shoestring Catch and Diving Drill
The use of a whiffle ball-tossing machine along with strategically placed
wrestling mats on a gym floor can make these catches both fun and safe.

In trying to produce a line drive, however, a slight downward swing
is needed. Beginning with a lower toss, contact the ball a little below the
waistline with the bat targeted at the fourth ring down. This will usually
produce just the right backspin to result in a line drive type of hit. If the
ball is instead contacted at the middle ring, a hard ground ball will result.

Coaches cringe when they see some of their hitters lunging, but they
are often guilty of the same mistake when they swing a fungo bat.
Lunging takes place when a hitter strides and swings at the same time. As
a result, he loses power and will also find himself way out in front of any
off-speed pitch. Since a fungo hitter is tossing the ball up to hit himself, he
doesn't have to worry about being fooled by the "pitch." However, if he
merely strides slightly while simultaneously swinging, *he is lunging* and is
losing leverage, power, and distance.

You must preface this action with a stride forward with your back leg
behind your front leg. This doubles the length of the stride and assures the
hands to be back in good hitting position. A longer, more powerful swing
will also result from the greater trunk rotation caused by the hips being

pointed further back following the first stride step. Remember, the ball is tossed up to hit following that first stride step, not during or before.

While diving for sinking liners to an outfielder's left or right is not a common play, an outfielder can be prepared indoors for this sometimes game-breaking play. Once again, by using wrestling mats, the outfielder can gain confidence in this play by meeting with success in diving left and later right when the drill is reversed. The balls are thrown by the coach or directed by him using any type of ball-throwing machine that can be made to consistently direct the ball to descend where needed atop the mat. Players soon gain confidence and realize the key importance of the extended elbow as mentioned earlier. It would be foolish to risk injury trying to practice the diving catch outdoors. This indoor drill, then, will hopefully go a long way in preparing for those miracle diving catches when outfielders are provided the opportunity in games.

The catch or leap at the fence is a fun situation for the players to practice. They love the opportunity to go as high as possible to deprive the coach's towering shots from clearing the fence. It's a chance to be a hero, even if it's only practice. After the coach has explained the several necessary techniques, the players are situated across the outfield. One at a time, the coach fungoes a long drive to each. The outfielders are allowed to take nothing more than a medium-depth position so that a long run back toward the fence will be necessary. Meanwhile, the coach hits from a distance that will allow his drives to occasionally clear the fence. An extra manager or player will be needed on the other side to retrieve those " home run" shots. With success in practice, players will soon find themselves making more and more of these miracle catches in critical game situations.

Finally, whenever a difficult sun is present, some fly ball practice must be provided. What better way to practice sun field techniques than to go through some of these same drills when the sun is shining brightly. Of course, the drill must be preceded by the coach's explanation of proper techniques. These techniques should include tips not only for shading the sun but for proper sunglass wear too. If conditions permit, all outfielders should be placed in the field where the sun would present the greatest problem. The coach may wish his outfielders to use their sunglasses for some of the drills. For the others, correct hand-and-glove-shading techniques would be encouraged. Soon, all the outfielders will have achieved newfound confidence in handling this nasty environmental condition.

Chapter 7

Mechanics of the Thrown Ball

INTRODUCTION

While the catch of a fly ball will retire the batter, it can also set in motion a confrontation between the outfielder and a runner who is hoping to advance after the catch. Following hits, runners will obviously advance one base, but another confrontation presents itself when a runner tries for a two- or three-base advance. Which will win out—the outfielder's arm or the runner's legs?

A strong arm is a God-given gift and is one of the prerequisites of a truly great outfielder. Over the relatively short course of a baseball season, little can be done to improve the actual strength of the arm. Yet, runners are constantly being thrown out by outfielders with lesser arms. Why? In some cases, the runner is simply being overaggressive to the point of being foolhardy. In other instances, though, the out call results from a well-developed throwing style, including a quick release and a well-positioned body at the time of the catch.

To begin, the ball should never be held after a catch with any base(s) occupied. This only wastes valuable time. Rather, the outfielder should immediately throw the ball to the waiting infielder/relay man. To get into this important habit, he should assume that every runner will be trying to take the extra base, regardless of whether it's a fly ball or a hit. It is a generally accepted guideline that for every step taken by an outfielder to get rid of the ball, the runner will take two.

Even without runners on base, there is a psychological advantage to be gained by throwing a ball hard and well back into the infield. The opposition learns early of the outfielder's well-developed throwing style and quick release, whether he possesses a super-strong arm or not. He gives the opposition no encouragement to run on his arm when the situation might present itself later. These opportunities should be used to show off the arm. The ball should be thrown hard and on a line right at the chest of the receiving infielder. Besides providing a psychological edge, it's also a great warm-up for the real thing, which could come at any time.

Fielding hits and making follow-up throws are discussed in the next chapter. However, the techniques involved in those throws are, in large part, very similar to those used following the catch of a fly ball.

While catchers and infielders have a throwing style all their own, outfielders can learn a lot from a study of their pitchers' throwing forms, assuming that they throw overhand. To gain full thrust and maximum carry, they should use a full range of motion as the pitcher does in his delivery. This throwing motion encompasses a whole series of component parts that are analyzed in this chapter. To get started, however, it would be best to review some prerequisites to getting off that great throw.

PREREQUISITES FOR A GOOD THROW

Just as a good batting swing can be developed only when first preceded by a good stance, so too can a good throw result only when the body is well positioned. The characteristics of a well-positioned body and catch include several techniques that are needed before the ball ever enters the glove.

These prerequisites include a body that is moving into the ball from about two steps back on a routine fly. The body has also rounded off the ball and is facing the direction of the intended throw. As the ball comes down, the body is relaxed. Gritting teeth and then trying to throw too hard will only rush and upset the delivery.

The catch should be two-handed, of course, despite what is often seen on the major league level. There is no advantage to a one-handed catch of a routine fly ball, but there sure are a number of obvious disadvantages that need no mentioning here. The two hands, side by side, should be at eye level or higher as the catch is made. The ball should be "seen" into the mitt.

Finally, as mentioned earlier, the catch should be made just slightly to the glove-hand side of the body for several reasons. Experimenting will convince you that the further to the throwing-arm side the catch is attempted, the tenser the feel in the upper arm with the glove. However, the glove hand and arm are virtually tension-free when positioned slightly to the glove-hand side of the body. Infielders long ago discovered that the same is true when fielding ground balls. Softer, tension-free hands are found when grounders are fielded slightly to the glove side of the center line of the body. Less "give" is possible when the glove hand is tensed and extended far to the throwing side.

Timing is the other factor to consider. When the ball is caught too far to the throwing side of the body, a less-than-balanced crowhop results, producing a weaker throw. Further, because the arm has such a short distance to travel before the ball's release, it isn't given enough time to affect a full range of motion while the crowhop is taking place. This puts the throwing arm and leg slightly out of sync, which again adversely influences the strength of the throw. Each outfielder must come to feel just what is most natural for him, but in most cases, experimentation will find that the most comfortable and efficient glove position will be slightly to the glove side of the center line of the body.

THE ANATOMY OF THE THROWN BALL

Getting off a great throw takes a lot more than merely a physically strong arm. It requires the synchronization and meshing of a number of body parts including, but not restricted to, the throwing arm. For that reason, it is best to study the roles and mechanics of each of these parts one at a time.

The Throwing Hand, Fingers, and Grip

Whenever a two-handed catch is made, two advantages to the throwing hand are gained. First, the throwing hand is right where it's most needed to help close the mitt to prevent the ball from popping out. Second, the proximity of the hand to the ball makes for a quick exchange and provides a little more time to assume the best possible grip for the best possible carry. The grip of the ball is often overlooked, yet it's a key component to the three objectives sought in every throw: accuracy, carry, and true bounce.

As a fly ball is caught, the outfielder moves the nearby bare hand in quickly to grip the ball and then bring it out into the throwing position. Simultaneously, he rolls the fingers of the gripping hand over the ball within the pocket of the glove to gain a grip over the wide seams. The outfielder's mind has been trained to perform this necessary task spontaneously, without actually thinking about it. It all occurs within a tiny fraction of a second. A grip over the wide seams allows all four seams of the ball to rotate against the air, resulting in a straighter throw and a better carry (Photo 7-1). Pitchers sometimes throw a two-seamed fastball to produce movement, but this is a throwing technique outfielders want to avoid (Photo 7-2).

The finger spread on the ball may range from one-half to three-quarters of an inch. The ring finger is tucked under the ball, never atop or on the side of the ball. Anything resembling a three-fingered grip only creates drag (Photo 7-3). In fact, pitchers often use a three-fingered grip to produce an off-speed pitch.

PHOTO 7-1: Correct Four-Seam Grip
Four seams biting against the air have the
effect of producing greater control and
carry. The ring finger is kept as far beneath
the ball as comfortably possible.

PHOTO 7-2: Incorrect Two-Seam Grip
A two-seam grip is more difficult to
control, with floating or dipping often the
result.

**PHOTO 7-3: Incorrect Wide Finger Spread
and Incorrectly Placed
Ring Finger**
A finger spread of more than three-quarters
of an inch or a ring finger placed high on
the side of the ball will both diminish the
strength of the throw.

PHOTO 7-4: Correct Daylight Grip
For maximum velocity and carry, a loose grip is essential. This equates to some daylight showing between the ball and the hand, viewed laterally.

PHOTO 7-5: Incorrect Deep Grip
A deep grip is one that produces no daylight. Such a grip produces a change-up toss of less than maximum velocity and carry.

PHOTO 7-6: Correct "Fingers-on-Top" Release
Maximum carry is produced when the release is made with the fingers directly atop the ball.

The grip can't be deep. Daylight must be visible between the ball and the hand's "web" area located between the thumb and index finger (Photo 7-4). Again, this provides for better carry, because it allows the ball to be released with a good wrist snap. This is essential for a strong throw. Jamming the ball in tight is still another method that some pitchers use to create a change-up effect. This is the last result the outfielder wants to achieve with his throws (Photo 7-5).

To produce the best possible carry, the wrist snap achieved at the release begins and continues with the fingers kept above the ball (Photo 7-6). This is a must if full arm extension is to be maintained throughout the arm swing. If the fingers release the ball from anywhere but a directly overhand position, the ball will move, but laterally (Photo 7-7). When this happens, the ball tails away from the intended target. Furthermore, when thrown in toward a base on a bounce, a ball thrown with any amount of sidespin often skips toward one side. Good backspin is necessary for a true bounce, and this can result only from a strong, directly overhand throw.

The Legs, Feet, and Crowhop

By the time the bare hand begins gripping and grasping the ball, the legs, feet, and hips are already at work doing their part to get off a good throw. As already mentioned, the outfielder lays back about two steps after rounding off the ball. This way, he can generate some rhythm and forward momentum while awaiting the descent of the ball. He should never make the catch with "dead feet" while a runner is preparing to advance. To get the whole body into the throw, momentum as well as balance must be created and maintained. This is accomplished through some footwork known as a crowhop, of which there are three generally accepted methods.

Crowhop #1: The Hop Method

If the outfielder is right-handed, this first and most popular method of crowhopping requires that the catch be made with the left foot forward. To begin, he pushes off this left leg after the catch in a hoplike step with the right leg. It is a step not just forward, but with the right foot coming down in front of the left foot. At the same time, the throwing arm is extended back through its full range of motion. In hopping the right leg in front of the left, the right foot should be squared so that the "side" of that foot is facing the target. In so doing, the lead shoulder will momentarily be pointed at its target as it should. Then the throw is completed as the left foot comes forward and accepts the weight transfer from the right leg (Photo Series 7-8). The hop should resemble someone quick-stepping over a very low fence of perhaps six to ten inches. The outfielder should work on making the hop with fluidity, under control and in sync with the throwing-arm movement. Otherwise, an unbalanced throw will result, diminishing both its carry and accuracy. As the left leg executes the second and final step of the crowhop, it comes up like a pitcher's raised leg during his kick. This produces greater forward momentum and gets the body behind the throw. He can't afford to throw the ball with just his arm.

This first type of crowhop truly deserves the word "hop" in its name, for that's exactly what takes place. More momentum, and thus power, can be generated with this crowhop than with either of the two about to be described. It is the most popular form of crowhop, but it can also be the most difficult to control with respect to accuracy. Herein lies its one potential disadvantage. Those who use it must constantly fight the tendency to leave the glove-arm side of the body open somewhat. An accurate throw requires the glove-arm side to close to the extent that the straight line connecting the two shoulders is pointing at the target. Those who fail to close up sufficiently usually find themselves not turning their throwing-side foot enough. Upon release of the ball, this foot must be perpendicular to the line of flight, rather than at a 45-degree angle. Those finding the "hopping" crowhop uncomfortable or too difficult to master may opt for another method.

Crowhop #2: The Glide-and-Skip Method

A second type of crowhop that works equally well relies more on a "skip" than a "hop" to produce the necessary momentum. It is used by a number of fine outfielders. Again, the catch is made by the right-handed outfielder with his left foot forward. As the catch is made, instead of pushing off the left leg and high stepping with the right, the outfielder begins the skipping crowhop by first stepping forward with the right foot. It is not a high step at all, but as the right foot is moving forward to take

PHOTO SERIES 7-8: The "Hop" Crowhop

This is the most popular and widely used of the three types of crowhops. It generates the greatest body momentum in the shortest amount of time.

(a)   (b)

(c)

this step, the right foot begins to turn out to help close the non-throwing side of the body as in the hopping crowhop. While this foot may not be turned completely perpendicular to the intended line of flight when the foot hits down, the foot turn is completed when a short and low skip is executed by this same foot. The skip raises the foot just enough for the spikes to clear the turf. All the while, the arm is extending back through a

PHOTO SERIES 7-9: The "Glide-and-Skip" Crowhop

The high hop of the first method is replaced by a longer glide step by the right leg, followed by a skip on that same leg. While time is sacrificed, accuracy is usually gained.

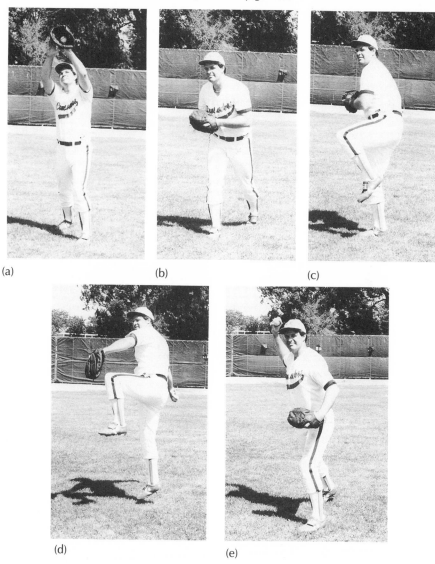

(a)
(b)
(c)

(d)
(e)

full range of motion into throwing position (Photo Series 7-9). Instead of using a high hop and throw as in the first method, a longer right-leg glide step and skip are used in this second crowhop method. The distance covered by the throwing-side foot from the moment of the catch to the moment of release should be about the same with either method. Because of its skip ingredient, which the hop method lacks, the glide-and-skip method requires just a split second longer to get the ball away. Despite this very slight drawback, it remains a fine and very acceptable method. Its value lies in the way it facilitates the necessary turn-in of the body, thus producing greater accuracy.

Crowhop #3: The Moon-Step Method

A third crowhop technique used by a number of outfielders with success is one that utilizes neither a hop nor a glide and skip. Again, the right-handed outfielder makes the catch with his left leg forward. His next movement, however, involves moving his right foot behind and to the left of his left foot. It resembles the footwork of a coach as he fungoes a ground ball. Not as much momentum can be generated as with either of the first two methods described due to the limited movement of this right leg. However, because of its mechanics, this method *immediately* places the right foot into the properly angled position for the throw. It also instantly closes the non-throwing side of the body and points the front shoulder at the target. After the right foot has moved behind and to the left of the left foot, the left leg moves forward to complete the movement.

As with the other methods, the arm is moved back through its full range of motion during the first step. Then, just as the left foot is completing the second step of the movement, the arm comes forward, and the ball is released (Photo Series 7-10). This third method is sometimes nicknamed the "moon-step crowhop." This method is a good choice for the outfielder who is already gifted with a strong arm, but is looking to improve his accuracy and shorten his release time. On the other hand, those looking for greater carry and strength behind their throws would better opt for one of the other methods.

The Lead Shoulder and Hip

Regardless of the crowhop used, the lead shoulder and hip must move and turn efficiently. To begin, the right foot, whether "hopping," "gliding and skipping," or "moon stepping," must be positioned so that the side of the right foot is facing its target. This foot turn somewhat resembles that of a pitcher when he pivots on the rubber just prior to his leg kick. To position the foot this way, the outfielder simultaneously turns the body outward. This action will curl in the left or lead shoulder for the right-handed outfielder, thus pointing it toward its target. He then drives off this foot to complete the crowhop movement.

If instead, the chest is pointed forward, the first step of the crowhop would find the toes of the throwing-side foot pointed at the target. This would make it impossible to produce maximum forward drive.

PHOTO SERIES 7-10: The "Moon-Step" Crowhop
While lacking the momentum-producing hop or glide, this method immediately places the throwing-side foot at the best possible angle for an
accurate throw.

(a)   (b)   (c)

(d)   (e)

As the ball is released on the last step of the crowhop, the outfielder
opens the lead hip sufficiently to prevent the chance of throwing across the
body (Photo 7-11). Otherwise, the throw will be stunted and will cause the
ball to tail (Photo 7-12). A good rule of thumb is to open the lead hip and

PHOTO 7-11: Correctly Opened Lead Hip Nearing the Release
The opening of the lead hip is accompanied by the pointing of the toes of the lead foot toward the target. This allows for a good follow-through.

PHOTO 7-12: Incorrectly Closed Lead Hip Nearing the Release
A closed hip at the time of release forces the outfielder to make his throw across the body. This reduces the ball's velocity and causes it to tail to the outfielder's right. Notice that the toes are pointed away from the target.

stride foot sufficiently to allow the belly button to point in the direction of the throw. An improper hand-release position and failure to completely open the lead shoulder constitute the two greatest causes of laterally inaccurate throws.

The Throwing Arm

Arm strength can see its potential realized only with directly overhand throws. With the elbow kept high, the outfielder creates an overhand spin that will cause the ball to "hang up" longer. Balls released with the least amount of lateral spin will sink less quickly. To produce a worthwhile overhand throw requires that the arm stay away from the body and be brought back through a complete range of motion. Never should the throw be short-armed. It will only shorten the throw.

Meanwhile, the glove hand and arm also serve a function. They provide for both accuracy and good body momentum by stretching forward at the same time that the throwing arm is being brought back. At that point, the line through the outfielder's shoulders should be parallel to the ground (Photo 7-13). Then, as his throwing arm begins to come forward, the glove hand begins to rotate downward to a point just outside the right-hander's left knee. It is important that the direction taken by the glove hand be downward, not out to a side, since this can throw the shoulder off-target.

PHOTO 7-13: Elbow-to-Elbow Straight Line
As the arm is brought back, the glove hand and arm are extended forward. This produces a straight line between the shoulders that is pointed at the target at that instant.

The Stride and Follow-Through

The release of the ball occurs on the last step of the outfielder's crowhop movement. This step is also known as the stride. At this point, the back foot push-off must be as hard as possible so that the entire body follows through to get the maximum strength behind the throw.

The stride should be kept short enough to allow the body to get into good throwing position with the arm up on top. At the release, the outfielder drives his body down and hard toward its target. This will allow for the arm to be traveling at full speed, too, thus assuring good velocity.

Similar to the pitcher, the outfielder must reach out and over toward the opposite foot as if trying to pick up grass. At the same time, his glove hand rotates downward to a point just outside the glove-side knee. With far too many outfielders, both arms and hands have taken these suggested routes, but they are drastically *decelerating!* This shouldn't be happening any more than a runner should be slowing down as he tags first base. Just as a runner must "run through the bag," the outfielder must continue to rotate his outstretched glove both down *and back up* out of sight behind him, without any deceleration.

The throwing hand should similarly not be slowing down as it reaches out, down, and across, but it should *snap back up* slightly as if trying to catch the glove hand. Only in this way can the thrower be assured that his arm is *still accelerating* as the ball is released. He wants to be like the baserunner whose body should be accelerating as he tags the bag, not leveling off or slowing down. With these techniques incorporated

PHOTO 7-14: The "Reach Out,
Down, and
Through"
Follow-Through
The stride is kept short and the throwing shoulder low. The throwing hand reaches down and across toward the opposite foot as does a pitcher.

into the throwing style of the outfielder, a maximum carry will follow (Photo 7-14).

THE TARGET AND TRAJECTORY

Every throw is targeted for either a relay man or an infielder at a base. To hit either target, the outfielder throws directly overhand following the crowhop with the toes of the lead foot pointing in the direction of the target. To further avoid tailing, he keeps the two fingers held across the wide seams of the ball atop the ball and not off to a side. His eyes are glued on a target such as the nose of the relay man. With throws to a relay man, the target and trajectory are a simple matter. Spotting the relay man should be easy enough if his two hands are raised. A hard-thrown ball should hit the relayman in the area that extends from the chest to the face. In addition, the ball should be thrown on the glove side to facilitate a possible follow-up throw. Arching a "lollipop" throw will only reduce its velocity and increase the chance of an overthrow. If a low, hard throw is underthrown, it can still be handled.

Where confusion often exists is with the throws to the bases. Outfielders are often unsure whether they are expected to get the throw in to the infielder at the base on a fly or on a bounce. Ideally, it would be great if every throw could come in hard and low on a fly. Unfortunately, most arms aren't strong enough to make this a reality and, sometimes too, the distance between the outfielder and the base is just too prohibitive for such a long throw.

When distance and/or arm strength make it impossible to get a hard, low throw in on a fly, the outfielder should try to bounce it in on one big bounce rather than letting loose with an arching throw too high to be cut off. Such high, arching throws are acceptable only when no follow-up play exists.

For instance, with a lone runner on base trying to advance following the catch of a fly ball, the relay man serves little purpose. Since cutting off a weak throw wouldn't help, why not let the outfielder give it the "old college try"?

In most cases, however, where an alternate play following a cutoff is possible, the one-bounce throw is the smart play to make. Of course, this doesn't give the outfielder free rein to short-hop the infielder who should be able to look forward to a reasonably good hop to handle. Then, too, with shorter throws, there should be no problem getting it there on a fly, hard and low. If the outfielder attempts to make the ball arrive on one bounce, the ball should ideally pass the cut-man between the chest and face with the shoulder being the ideal target. The cut-man must come to know the arm strengths of his outfielders so he can set up at the ideal distance between the outfielder and the base. Assuming that the cut-man has aligned himself properly, the outfielder needn't think about throwing to the base itself. Instead, he just throws for the cut-man's shoulders. If the throw is allowed to go through, it should arrive at the base on one long bounce. This is the outfielder's throwing-target goal.

THE REVERSE PIVOT

In a tag-up situation, an outfielder would like nothing better than having enough time to round the ball, move into it as the catch is made, crowhop, and throw. This is the ideal situation. Oftentimes, though, he must make the catch following a hard and long run laterally to the glove side. After such a catch, it's very difficult to get off a quick throw against an advancing runner. This is because the conservative approach is to brake with the glove-side leg, planting that leg, opening up to the target, and throwing (Photo Series 7-15). However, this method involves too much inefficient turning. It takes too much time. The body's momentum has a tough time trying to understand in what direction it's supposed to be going. By the time it does get on track, a valuable split second or more has been lost. A runner, trying to tag up and advance after a catch, will too often be successful.

Stopping such a runner with greater consistency requires that the outfielder use a technique that will provide better balance. It will also make better use of the momentum that went into the catch. This much-needed quicker and more efficient technique is known as a reverse pivot.

The reverse pivot can be used by the outfielder whenever he is moving fast and hard laterally to the glove side. As the fly ball is caught, he plants the leg opposite the throwing arm and opens the body toward the glove side. This necessitates a complete turn of the back to the infield. Then, a whirl and throw to the target off of the throwing-side leg completes the play (Photo Series 7-16). With this more efficient method, the momentum behind the throw makes it quicker and stronger. However, there are two drawbacks to this method.

First, because the body makes a 180-degree turn, the eyes momentarily lose sight of their target. Coming out of the turn, the outfielder must pick up the targeted base or relay man quickly so additional steps won't be necessary.

Second, the reverse pivot actually consists of a long, horizontal step that aids in reducing sideward momentum. It gets the body balanced quickly for the throw. From this position, it's very easy and tempting to drop the hand or elbow or simply even to move the fingers from the proper

PHOTO SERIES 7-15: Traditional Pivot Following a Running Catch to the Glove Side

The outfielder needs a minimum of four steps to get rid of the ball.

(a)   (b)

(c)   (d)

"on top" position. What results is a weak and tailing three-quarters or even sidearm throw. Using the reverse pivot is never an excuse for not keeping the arm raised with a high elbow for a good overhand release. With drillwork, though, these drawbacks can be overcome.

PHOTO SERIES 7-16: Reverse Pivot Following a Running Catch
to the Glove Side

After the catch, the outfielder turns his back to the infield and brakes with a long, horizontal step. He will then be able to get off his throw in as few as just two steps.

(a)   (b)

(c)   (d)

DRILLS AND METHODS OF INSTRUCTION

Drills involved with the rudiments of throwing are usually not met with the same kind of enthusiasm as those that involve catching a fly ball. Tracking down fly balls is fun. Throwing a baseball for accuracy as well as distance is more challenge and work than fun. Outfielders seem to be more interested in their putout total than in any pursuit of assists. A number of reasons may contribute to this phenomenon.

First, many players feel that their throwing style is just fine. Why tamper with it? After all, they have been throwing this way all their lives and few, if any, negative comments have been directed their way.

Second, ballplayers feel that over the short course of a season, little can be done to improve the God-given strength of their throwing arm. Strength-training programs take a lot of time.

Finally, when it comes to throwing out a runner following a catch or even a hit, scoring rules place outfielders under far less pressure than infielders. When a runner is able to tag up and score from third on even a short fly to the outfield, the blame is usually directed at the pitcher who allowed the batter to hit the ball that far. If an infielder's throw to first on a routine play pulls the first baseman off the bag, it's ruled an error, of course. However, what happens on the short fly ball to an outfielder with the runner tagging at third? If the throw home appears to have beaten the runner but is thrown wide allowing the runner to score, no error is charged. Again, most of the blame is directed at the pitcher. Preceding any drills, then, the coach must convince his players of several points.

First, while they may have been throwing their own unique way for some time, that doesn't mean it's the best way or that improvement can't be found. Outfielders have been neglected long enough. If they have a coach willing to analyze their throwing style, make recommendations, and help them, they should welcome such help with open arms.

Second, it's true that a training program to improve arm strength takes more time than is available during the baseball season However, what the coach is striving for is just some "fine tuning" to improve efficiency. It may be something in the grip, throwing-arm mechanics, crowhop, or follow-through that needs a complete change or tiny adjustment. What's important is that each outfielder improve to that point where he can truly say he is throwing as "efficiently" as possible in light of his God-given arm strength.

Finally, outfielders must be made to understand that their role and importance is not only in catching fly balls, but also in contributing with strong and accurate throws to the bases. Any outfielder assist is one of the most beautiful and dramatic defensive plays in a game. The coach should keep his outfielders in friendly competition with each other for the team lead in outfield assists and post that statistic prominently with the others. Equipped with such pride in their newfound and efficient throwing motion, outfielders will soon find greater motivation in assisting on a greater number of putouts on the bases. With such an understanding of what the coach is trying to accomplish, outfielders will come to look upon throwing drills with a greater sense of purpose and enthusiasm.

Indoor Drills

As mentioned in Chapter 2, the gym is a great pre-season site for analyzing outfielders' throwing mechanics. You can begin by just observing your outfielders play catch and checking the grip used by each. You may want to ask each to "freeze" during his throwing motion to check for proper finger placement in the grip. Check also to see that the fingers stay atop the ball and not off to a side. A grip across the seams will avoid sliderlike throws that result from a finger placement along the seams rather than across them. Watch for a fully extended arm, which should be preceded by the palm of the throwing hand passing by the thigh. An arm extended back fully to its limit provides the throw with greater power and distance. A crisp wrist snap should be observed, which, in turn, should lead to a follow-through characterized by a reaching-down motion as well as a "heel kick to the sky." As the drill continues, remind the players to emphasize these techniques in their throwing styles.

In addition, the hip, lead shoulder, lead foot, and stride should also be carefully watched and scrutinized within the larger framework of the entire throw. Once outdoors, it becomes possible to emphasize the lengthening of the throwing distance to 120 feet.

Use of the Knee Catch Drill (described in Chapter 2) works well indoors to emphasize the importance of the finger position, hip and trunk rotation, and wrist snap.

The Long Toss Drill (also described in Chapter 2) helps in all these areas as well, but can be utilized only outdoors unless a fieldhouse or similar indoor facility is available.

So far this chapter has discussed throws to the bases following the catch of a fly ball. Now, all the throwing techniques discussed and drilled so far must get blended with a highly efficient crowhop. Teaching, demonstrating, and drilling crowhops works quite well indoors. After explaining the techniques of each of the three variations along with the pros and cons, allow the outfielders to crowhop, one at a time, to identify the crowhop variation that each employs. The outfielders can then be drilled in getting off throws using each of the three variations of crowhops, working on one at a time.

For each type of crowhop, the outfielders might be asked to begin with the ball already in their gloves or may have it tossed to them by a partner-outfielder facing them from a distance of about 20 feet. Rounding off the ball to the outfielder's left or right can also be made a part of the drill. The throws may be made to a waiting infielder across the gym. The infielder then returns a throw to that same outfielder who then reverses position with his partner as the drill continues (Diagram 7-1). Utilizing three stations, six outfielders can drill simultaneously.

The reverse pivot method for making a catch and then releasing a throw quickly can be practiced indoors, too. The entire gym floor is needed for the outfielder to cover some ground laterally before making the catch. The throw is then made to a waiting infielder stationed near the coach at the other end of the gym. Because these make-believe fly balls can't be tossed too high, the coach may prefer to have the infielder make the tosses instead. The coach can then remain at the other end of the gym near the waiting outfielders. The tosses should be made to require right-handed outfielders to move to their left, while the left-handers would be

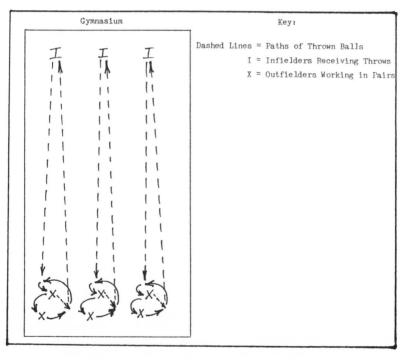

DIAGRAM 7-1:   Indoor "Round, Crowhop, and Throw" Drill
The outfielder making the throw to the infielder also receives the return throw while his partner positions himself for his turn.

made to move to their right. With all these throwing techniques better understood and drilled indoors, outfielders will find even greater improvement when these drills are moved outdoors onto a complete field, with the coach using a fungo bat or a flyball-tossing machine.

Outdoor Drills

Once out on the field, outfielders can be drilled under more realistic conditions and distances. How realistic the conditions become will depend upon the coach. A coach lacking creativity will often just take a bat down the left field line and punch out soft flies to his group of outfielders huddled en masse somewhere in center field. It's no wonder these players develop a feeling that their position is taken for granted.

When practicing throws following the catch of a fly ball, consider these ideas.

First, use the actual outfield. Just as infielders expect to be drilled from their familiar infield positions, so too should outfielders be stationed in the outfield of the diamond. This gives them a better perspective of their targets and throwing distances. You may wish to drill just three outfielders at a time by placing one in each field, or you may wish to drill your entire outfield squad with, at most, two in each field. For some drills, you may wish to use a special column alignment of outfielders as is described later.

Second, use a fungo bat to provide extra distance and altitude to fly balls. There should be no excuse for not using this great tool. It produces greater efficiency with less effort.

Third, rather than shy away from outfield fly drills on windy or sunny days, look forward to such conditions to better prepare players for these game conditions. Even at practice, sunglasses or eye blackener should be encouraged on sunny days.

Fourth, in an effort to instill communication skills, ask the outfielder to call for every fly ball he goes after and several times, too. Any nearby outfielder should also be expected to communicate reassurance with words like, "You've got it," "All yours," "Nobody near you."

Fifth, unless throws are being confined to just one base, use a complete infield. All infielders will be needed as soon as cuts begin being made and thrown to different bases.

Sixth, the role of the relay/cut man can never be neglected. Never ask outfielders to make throws without a relay man present and aligned. Without a relay man present, the outfielder could be tempted to "lollipop" his throws to the bases. In actual ball games, such lofty throws prohibit cutoffs that could be redirected to another base.

Seventh, as an outfielder makes his catch, his catching and throwing techniques require close scrutiny. This includes a proper rounding of the ball, moving into the catch, a two-handed catch, a good crowhop, proper arm and body mechanics, and a fluid follow-through. Without the coach's corrections, the outfielder only fools himself into believing that his techniques are fine and need no refinement. Remember, practice does NOT make perfect. PRACTICING PROPER TECHNIQUES MAKES PERFECT!

Even more important at this stage of the play, however, is the accuracy of the throw. After all, the throw in this drill is our main focus. For that reason, an eighth idea might be to call out a grade for each throw. An "A" would require a line throw to the relay man's glove side at a height ranging from the eyes to the chest. A grade of "B" might allow the line throw to range from the top of the head to the waist or might require the relay man to adjust his position laterally a step or two to receive the throw on his glove side. A "C" grade might expand the allowable height of the throw to range from the relay man's maximum reach down to his shoe tops. A similar throw that also requires a lateral adjustment by the relay man would warrant a "D." Any lollipop throw, ball in the dirt or otherwise unreachable toss would receive an "F." Players love competition and will welcome such games to determine the first to reach a certain number, 21 for example.

To play such a game, award 4 points for an "A," 3 for a "B," 2 for a "C," and 1 for a "D." Of course, not all throws need to be cut off. Therefore, when throws are allowed to continue to the baseman, still award a grade based on the position of the relay man as the ball passes him. In fact, you may ask the relay man to assign the grade for each throw, while a manager tallies the points nearby.

An easier scoring system merely requires a certain number of "A's," like five, to be earned by an outfielder to win the game. Any throw warranting anything less than an "A" simply gets nothing. This may initially bring on some moans and groans when some good, but not great, throws fail to increase a player's score. Soon, though, the groans will change into more concentrated efforts to produce nothing less than perfect tosses. With more and more great throws will come greater and greater confidence and pride on the part of each outfielder. And those who finish near the bottom of these graded drills will also wake up to the reality that the recommended changes in technique might not be so bad after all.

Whether players are competing with each other for grades or not, there will be times when you will want all the throws directed to the same base or relay man. In this situation, two methods are suggested.

The first method involves an alignment of one outfielder behind the other in very deep center field. The outfielder in front of the line then moves up to a center fielder's normal position. There, he awaits the coach's first fungo shot. The fly balls should be mixed in direction, with about half sent to left-center and the other half to right-center. This provides good practice for circling into position and moving into the throw. Further, when an outfielder is running hard for a fly ball in a direction away from the base, encourage him to execute the reverse pivot technique. Of course, this can only be done when a right-handed outfielder is moving to his left or when a left-handed outfielder is moving to his right. The reverse pivot allows for the throw to be made in a minimum of time. Whether the outfielder reverse pivots or rounds the ball off in the conventional manner, he must get his body positioned to be facing the relay man or the target base. After handling the fly ball hit to him, the player moves to the back of the line in deep center field and awaits his next turn (Diagram 7-2).

A second method of aligning outfielders for group throwing drills is accomplished by first splitting them into two groups. One group is stationed in deep left-center field one behind the other, while the other group is aligned the same way in deep right-center field. With about six

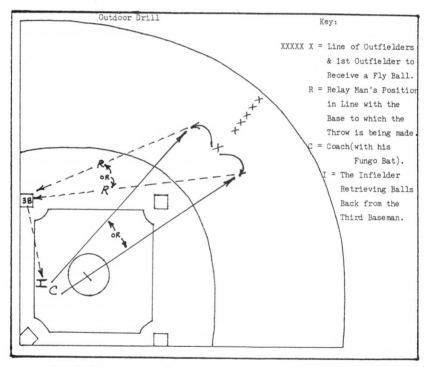

DIAGRAM 7-2:   Outdoor "Round, Crowhop, and Throw" Drill
The outfielders are instructed to use a reverse pivot whenever
the occasion allows.

outfielders on a team, this would make for two lines of three outfielders each. The front man in each line then moves forward to assume an average depth position in left-center and right-center field.

The coach next fungoes a fly ball to straightaway center field. The left-center fielder calls for the ball as he moves to his left to round off the ball. Making the catch, he then throws toward the relay man and the base designated prior to the drill. The outfielder then moves to the rear of the line of right-center fielders. Meanwhile, the outfielder from right-center field has been providing words of assurance to the outfielder who called for the ball. In addition, he backs up the play as he would in a game. After the play, he moves to the back of the line of left-center fielders.

Having the two lines alternating catches provides both groups the opportunity to approach fly balls from both directions. For that reason, both left- and right-handed outfielders will be able to use an occasional reverse pivot. This way, everyone receives practice in moving in both

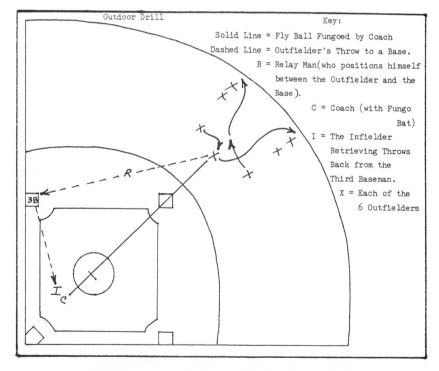

DIAGRAM 7-3:   Outdoor "Fly Ball - Weave" Drill
Fly ball communication skills, backup responsibilities, and plenty of running and throwing are all contained in this simple but comprehensive drill.

directions to round off fly balls and make a follow-up throw toward a base. This drill also provides the other outfielder involved in the play with drillwork in fly ball communication and backup responsibilities. Because four of the participants are almost always in motion, either tracking a fly ball or moving toward the end of the opposite line, the drill doubles as a fine conditioner, too. The diagram here shows the throws being made toward third base, but second base or home will work almost as well (Diagram 7-3).

These drills along with their numerous variations and modes of operation should convince outfielders of the importance not only of the catch itself, but also of every minute mechanic preceding and following that catch. They will also come to understand and appreciate the role and importance of the relay/cut man. Their motivation toward these ends will be enhanced by the commitment demonstrated by their coach's use of so much time and such a variety of drills to accomplish these goals.

Chapter 8

Fielding Hits and Follow-up Throws

INTRODUCTION

In this chapter, we study the outfielder's handling of base hits; some of these will be rather routine line drives, humped-back liners, or just hard-hit ground balls that have eluded the infielders. While most will take a rather direct route to the outfielder, there will be some that require a lot of lateral movement to get to the ball. Still others will become extra base hits as they enter the alleys or rebound off the fences.

Every outfielder likes nothing better than to track down some lazy fly ball hit his way, but sooner or later he will be called upon to field every type of outfield hit imaginable. Speed and aggressiveness will certainly be needed along with a mechanically correct and efficient fielding technique. Together, these talents will combine to corral the ball quickly and sure-handedly.

Most hits are fielded using the same mechanical technique used by infielders. Sometimes, though, specialized scooping or one-knee techniques provide better options for certain conditions and strategies. All these techniques are discussed in the next several pages.

Finally, how may all these techniques and strategies best be driven into the minds of the players to make their execution second nature? What drills can the coach use to get these points across? All of these base-hit fielding concepts and drillwork are now the center of attention.

FIELDING BASE HITS

Base hits to the outfield fall into one of three categories. There are, of course, the direct hits which probably comprise at least one-half of all hits to the outfield. Then there are the shots that require a hard lateral run to track down and, finally, the shots that reach the fence and rebound. As a result, a one-two-three set of procedural steps is impossible to state for fielding these hits. Yet, there are certain common goals for outfielders to consider and strive to attain for all hits. They include quickness in getting to the ball, a sure-handed pickup, and good body positioning to aid in the upcoming throw. Failure to achieve even one of these will usually result in one or more additional bases being garnered by each baserunner. More detailed procedures depend upon the type of hit involved.

DIRECT HITS

Most direct hits are hard or soft liners well outside the reach of any infielder. Others, though, will be perceived as ground balls that an infielder will be able to get to and handle flawlessly. But outfielders should never allow themselves to think this way, nor to be surprised when a ground ball eludes an infielder, whether it be a hit or an error. As each ground ball comes off a bat, they should treat it as one that will find its way into the outfield. This way, no hesitation will result.

With every direct hit, the outfielder's first thought and course of action must be that of charging the ball. Waiting for the ball to reach him rather than moving to the ball as quickly as possible represents the opposite of quickness and defensive aggressiveness. Runners are taught to be aggressive by rounding the base hard. They are taught to think in terms of taking an extra base if the outfielder provides them with the least excuse for doing so. Failure to charge the ball is certainly one such excuse.

Charging the ball satisfies five very related desires:

1. It demonstrates aggressiveness in one's play.
2. It brings the outfielder and ball together more quickly.
3. It allows the outfielder greater time to assume a good grip and body position in preparation for a throw when that runner does try for the extra base.
4. It discourages the opposition from running on an outfielder.
5. It substantially reduces the distance required for an upcoming throw. This kind of hustle can shorten a throw by as much as 30 feet.

However, the outfielder should take care to avoid charging the ball too hard. Failure to do so may cause him to bobble the ball, overrun it, or force a rushed throw, resulting in an errant one. The remedy involves getting the body under control by slowing down about six feet from the ball. In the process, he does not stop, but he does resort to short jab steps. This slowdown is reminiscent of the middle infielder who rushes toward second base to take a throw from another infielder to begin a double play.

Attaining complete body control places him in a totally balanced state. Simultaneously, it readies the body and glove to lower into proper fielding position, which is imperative for a sure-handed catch.

While an outfielder's first thought may be that of charging the ball on a direct hit in his direction, his second thought regards the actual pickup of the ball. There are three techniques that may be used. These include: (1) the infielders' method, (2) the one-knee-drop method, and (3) the do-or-die scoop method. The method chosen will generally depend upon the field conditions, speed of the batter-runner, and the game situation.

The Infielders' Method

This is the most common method used today, especially when the outfield area is level, dry, and well kept. The outfielder plays the ball directly in front of him just as an infielder would do. Unless the situation calls for the ball to be fielded off to the side of the body using the "Scoop Method" (which is discussed later), he makes contact with the ball where his body can help block it in case the ball bounds off or over his glove. Of course, before contact is made, the outfielder charges the ball aggressively, bringing his body under control about six feet before contact is made. In so doing, his body movement is slowed appreciably but not stopped completely. Rather, his body should find itself gliding smoothly into position to field the ball rather than taking on a "quick dip" appearance as the ball arrives.

A bouncing ball should be contacted preferably at the top of its hop or, as the second best choice, on its short hop immediately after contacting the ground on one of its bounces. It's at the in-between positions of the bounce that contact should be avoided if at all possible. These will almost always cause fits and often errors for an outfielder.

In gliding into the infielders' stance for the combination rolling/bouncing base hit, the outfielder's feet should be slightly staggered, with the throwing-side leg back one to six inches (Photo 8-1). This position will best prepare the outfielder to move into the crowhop phase of the entire action. Fielding the ball in the toe-to-toe position that may work well for some infielders is not recommended for outfielders.

He bends in both the knees and waist, with the back almost parallel to the ground. To look the ball into the glove, both the buttocks and head must be down. Looking up to catch sight of the runner before the ball has entered the glove accounts for a large number of bobbles seen in the outfield. The ball must be caught before a target is determined for any upcoming throw.

He extends both hands, not just the glove hand, down and forward to await the ball. As with the fly ball, trying to make a one-handed catch of a

**PHOTO 8-1: Infielders' Method for
Ground Balls**
Except when strategy dictates otherwise,
the outfielder should field base hits with
the same style and mechanics used by
infielders.

rolling ball prevents the bare hand from moving into the pocket of the
glove quickly to both secure the catch and gain a quick and correct across-
the-seams grip. With just one hand down, the tendency is to look up just
before the ball and glove make contact. Having both hands down, open,
and extended solves all these potential problems. Further, with hands
extended, a bad bounce gives those hands some room to move back in
toward the body and readjust. However, when the hands are down, but
not extended, this room for adjustment doesn't exist. The legs will only get
in the way of the backward-moving elbows that are trying to find room in
that split second to readjust to the bad hop. This also happens when
insufficient time is given to get the body under control after the charge of
the ball. By trying to dip down quickly on the run, he contacts the ball
beneath him instead of out in front. This makes it virtually impossible to
look the ball all the way into the glove. So, unless the ball luckily smacks
into the center of the pocket of the glove, a bobble is likely to follow.

It is also important that the outfielder contact the ball on the glove-
side half of the body. On that side, it is so much easier to leave the glove
arm relaxed and the glove hand open. The further to the right that the
glove is placed down, the more difficult it will be to do both. Either the arm
will remain relaxed but the glove will provide only a small target with a
partially closed look, or the glove will remain open at the expense of a
tensed forearm. By fielding the ball on the glove side of the body, he will
also facilitate his search for rhythm in the crowhop and throw. The

infielder begins his crowhop and throw from an almost stationary position, but the outfielder's body is moving a bit faster at this point. For that reason, he must work at controlling his body speed regardless of the crowhop method employed. Without such control, most throws will overshoot their targets. At one time or another, everyone has witnessed a hurried throw to the place that not only eluded the catcher's outstretched mitt but perhaps the entire backstop as well!

The best cure, of course, is prevention. That means, once again, getting the body under control by slowing it down about six feet short of the contact point. However, when this hasn't occurred for whatever reason, the outfielder still has recourse to a second choice remedy. If using the hop or glide-and-skip method of crowhop, the outfielder raises his body off the ground higher than usual during the first step of the crowhop. That is, the vertically upwards movement of the body is exaggerated in an attempt to slow down the body, enabling the arm to release a more controlled throw. Those using the moon-step method of crowhop will be unable to use this maneuver but may, through practice, learn to take a moon step of longer length, which will produce the same slowdown of the body. The crowhop and throw are otherwise mechanically the same as for the action following the catch of a fly ball, described in Chapter 7.

The One-Knee-Drop Method

Despite its many advantages, the infielders' method for fielding direct hits sometimes wisely takes a back seat to a second technique known as the "One-Knee-Drop" Method. The characteristics of this safety-first method are designed to handle some unique field conditions and game situations. These include the following:

1. Rough, poorly groomed outfield surfaces.
2. A wet grass surface.
3. No one on base and a non-threatening batter-runner, such as a slow runner or most pitchers.
4. Non-crucial, non-gambling, and non-do-or-die situations.

Basically, this second method of fielding a direct hit is used as a precaution against a possibly tricky hop, especially on a bad outfield surface. It also protects against a ball that is apt to skid on a wet outfield. The one-knee-drop method begins with the ball being charged. Again, the outfielder must bring his body under control with choppy steps to slow down shortly before the ball arrives. It may also be necessary to round the ball, too, if the hit is angled to the left or right. This gets the body facing its intended target at the moment of contact with the ball. It also provides for a quick release and accurate throw just as it does following the catch of a fly ball. When a lot of lateral movement is required, this method won't do, unless the outfielder is willing to concede a two-base hit. The one-knee-drop method is best used with direct or near-direct hits.

As the outfielder goes down into position to await the ball, he drops down to one knee (Photo 8-2). It is the knee on the throwing side that goes down. The other leg (left leg for the right-handed outfielder) is stretched and angled slightly to the outside to make room for the glove and glove arm. As with the infielders' method, the ball must be looked into the glove and both hands used. In this technique, a fine "blocking" position has been established with virtually no room for the ball to skip by. However, this big advantage must be weighed carefully in light of the method's disadvantages.

If the ball bounces badly to the left or right, the outfielder is in a difficult position from which to recover. Note that the glove-hand elbow is already in contact with the "up" knee, leaving it with no maneuverability to the glove side. It also becomes more difficult to get the two hands extended as far out in front as with the infielders' method.

Unfortunately, the ball is fielded from a "dead" position, thus sacrificing whatever body momentum may have been present prior to getting down onto the one knee. Consequently, it becomes tougher to come up throwing. Oftentimes, the faster runners will look for this opportunity

PHOTO 8-2: One-Knee-Drop Fielding Method
Field conditions are usually the determining factor in the use of this safer, but less aggressive method of fielding base hits.

to demonstrate their aggressiveness. The loss of momentum will affect the degree of power derived from the upcoming crowhop. The runner might not try taking an extra base just because the outfielder dropped to one knee, but will probably try to take it when this method is coupled with the slightest bobble. The key to successfully using the one knee-drop-method will lie in the outfielder's ability to pick the right spots for its use.

The Do-or-Die Scoop Method

A third method for fielding direct hits and some that are not so direct is the "Do-or-Die Scoop" Method. Because it involves fielding the ball off to the side of the body with one hand, this technique is also referred to as "the one-handed side pickup." The "do-or-die" nickname was tacked onto this method for its use when the game is on the line, often during the last inning of a close game. Yet, the amateur as well as the professional player has come to adopt this time-saving method more and more in non-critical situations as well. In fact, on the major league level, it is often used routinely whenever the outfielder has the opportunity. Still, the method is not recommended for the usual base hit for one very good reason: If the ball takes a crazy hop or the outfielder takes his eye off the ball, his body won't be there to block the ball. Instead of fielding a base hit, he may find himself chasing down a hit and a one- , two- , or three-base error. But the method does have some very worthwhile advantages and, if used with discretion, can become a valuable tool in fielding hits with the purpose of throwing out an advancing runner.

To minimize the disadvantages, the scoop method should wisely be reserved for use on nothing less than a dry, level, and well-groomed outfield where bad bounces will be the exception rather than the rule. Yes, the major league outfielder with his perfectly manicured grass or artificial turf is increasingly seen using this method for even the most routine of hits. However, most outfielders would be well advised to limit its use to certain "made-for" situations.

Certainly, this includes the scenario of the tie ball game in the last inning with the winning run trying to score from second base on a base hit to the outfield. For sure, this is the ultimate do-or-die situation. All caution is thrown to the wind here even if the game is being played on a less-than-ideal turf. However, with at least a mediocre outfield turf, this better-named scoop method may be used in an attempt to retire less important runners at the plate. It may also be used to gun down a runner trying to move from first to third on a base hit or during a hit-and-run play when the lead runner will undoubtedly be trying to advance the extra base.

The scoop method represents a time-saver for the outfielder. When it's used, it is because the outfielder hopes that the time saved in getting to the ball will make the needed difference in throwing out the advancing runner. He will be able to charge the ball harder and, therefore, get to it more quickly. Yet, as with the other methods, taking some jab steps will be necessary to get the body under control. Otherwise, he'll either have to take a couple of extra steps after contacting the ball or pay the price with a wild throw. While the extra steps might produce a more accurate throw, the time-saving advantage will have been lost. Like the maxim, for each step taken by the outfielder, the runner takes two.

The scoop method begins like the infielders' method with a hard charge for the ball followed by a couple of jab steps for better body control as the ball is approached. In so doing, he slows down as needed. Again, he glides into the ball by a bend in the knees and waist, but he allows only the glove hand to go down. This is the beneficial time-saver. It is so important for proper body control to bend well in both knees and not just at the waist in a stiff-legged, giraffelike fashion. Then, with the back parallel to the ground, the eyes look the ball all the way into the glove. The eyes must actually see the ball secure in the pocket of the glove before looking up.

As can be seen with the right-handed outfielder in Photo Series 8-3, the ball contacts the glove just a few inches in front of and off to the side of the outfielder's left spike. As in catching a fly ball, the right-handed outfielder finds his left foot ahead of his right, placing him in an ideal position from which to begin his crowhop.

Following the pickup, he will usually want to use the most popular and efficient hop type of crowhop. Both feet find themselves off the ground as he closes his front shoulder while keeping his eyes on the target. He begins with a very pronounced vertical crowhop upward as well as forward. The upward thrust comes from a push off the left leg while the right leg then executes the upward hop. The crowhop, of course, is intended to produce balance by reducing his momentum. Yet, this momentum will not be reduced sufficiently if the crowhop emphasizes the forward movement instead of the vertical lift. It is not a broad jump at all, but more closely resembles a vertical leap. Without a distinctly vertical crowhop, the throwing arm won't have enough time to be elevated sufficiently to be in an ideal throwing position. The velocity will be lacking as well as the accuracy (usually high) resulting from the rushed throw.

Sometimes, when the outfielder fails to take the vertical crowhop, his subconscious instincts will tell him that he is not yet in good throwing position, and he will find himself taking an additional two steps before releasing the ball. Of course, valuable time is lost, thus bringing into question the use of the scoop method in the first place. Because the crowhop is executed within one second of time and must be accomplished with the use of mental muscle memory, the vertical component of the crowhop must be driven home through daily drill.

PHOTO SERIES 8-3: The "Do-or-Die" Scoop Method

Unless playing on a very well-groomed turf, this method should be used to halt the advance of a crucial runner only in a game-determining situation.

(a) (b) (c)

(d) (e)

    The glide-and-skip crowhop can also be used here but, by its very nature, as described in Chapter 7, will require a tiny bit of additional time for the skip before getting rid of the ball. This, again, contradicts the intention for which the outfielder is using the scoop method. The third type of crowhop, the moon-step variation, is the most awkward to execute with the scoop method. Yet, it can be mastered with practice as attested to by those professionals who use this method. It is difficult, but possible to master two different types of crowhops for use in these different situations.

The other components of every crowhop, including the pointing of the shoulder line at the target and the high kick follow-through, are every bit as applicable here as following the catch of a fly ball.

As the outfielder begins his charge for the ball with the scoop method in mind, it's because he knows that he'll be making a throw to a base to either retire an advancing runner or to dissuade a runner from trying for such an advance. When the ball is hit, he should have already surveyed the situation, being aware of the whereabouts of any and all baserunners. Then, upon looking up after fielding the ball, a split-second decision is made to either go after the lead runner, or instead concentrate on a throw to another base with a back runner in mind. This decision will be based upon many factors, just as was the case following the catch of a fly ball with one or more runners on base. The most determining factor, though, will be the position of the runners with respect to their target bases. Specific guidelines are given in the last chapter, which deals with throwing strategy.

HITS TO THE ALLEYS AND DOWN THE LINES

Base hits to the outfielder's left or right must not only be charged, but must also be rounded whenever possible. Just as with a fly ball, the base hit is best handled if fielded with the body facing home plate. This allows the throw to travel in the same direction as found in his body momentum. The slight adjustment needed to throw to third instead of home or second base is made as the crowhop begins. Again, the use of a couple of jab steps will get the player's speed under control and will prevent wild throws brought on by rushing.

Now, he quickly decides the method to use. It could be the conventional infielders' method, the slower but surer one-knee-drop method, or the quick but riskier scoop method.

Unless the base hit is relatively close by or unless the situation calls for blocking the ball at all costs, the one-knee-drop method would be the last choice. To move laterally a substantial distance, rounding the ball and then going down on one knee would most likely provide an extra base advance for all runners. That leaves the infielders' method and the scoop method. Which method to choose will depend, as mentioned earlier, upon field conditions, the anticipated actions of the runner(s), and the game situation.

Base hits requiring a long lateral run toward one of the alleys or down a line present some special problems. For one thing, the ball cannot be charged, at least not in a forward direction. Second, the ball can be rounded only by moving diagonally away from the plate and toward the deeper corners of the outfield.

As he begins his run for the ball, the outfielder must decide quickly whether to play it aggressively or conservatively. A ball hit down the line will usually result in a double unless the outfielder was playing him there. As a consequence, the outfielder should usually play the ball carefully by rounding it well, conceding the double unless the ball is fielded at a shallow distance. Care must be taken with the longer hit down the line that it not be haphazardly played into a triple through an outfielder's fruitless attempt to get the runner at second base. With a runner on first at the time, there remains a good chance to get that runner at the plate if he chooses to try to score on the play. But how important is that run? The game situation should provide that answer in a hurry. If it is not that important a run, then discretion should rule, resulting in the concession of a two-base hit and a simultaneous rounding of the ball if at all possible. If played conservatively, the scoop method will not be necessary nor should its use be chanced needlessly. Instead, the infielders' method or the one-knee-drop technique should be used.

If the decision is to field the ball aggressively, and if the ball has been hit to the outfielder's throwing-arm side, he should use the scoop method if possible. If not, he'll be forced to backhand the ball.

On the ball hit into the left-center-field or right-center-field gaps, the possibility of a double is far less certain due to the usually shorter throw needed. This provides all the more reason, then, to use the reverse pivot when chasing a ball into the gap to the outfielder's glove side. The saving of a split second can make the difference between a safe or an out call at second base. As first described in Chapter 7, the ball is fielded one-handed while running away from the infield. Then, one more step is taken by the throwing-side leg as the outfielder simultaneously prepares to brace against that same leg for the throw into the relay man. In the process, the right-hander's body has turned counterclockwise or the left-hander's body has turned clockwise. The movement, however, is more of a pivot than a turn (Photo Series 8-4). To get something on the throw, the elbow should be kept high and not allowed to drop as so often happens with a hurried throw.

PLAYING THE REBOUND OFF A FENCE

Occasionally, the outfielder will find himself chasing down a long drive rolling to a fence or bouncing off it. While it may not be a happy moment for the defense, he cannot allow himself to make the situation

PHOTO SERIES 8-4: Reverse Pivot Technique
This method is best used following a long lateral run to a ball hit into an
alley or down a baseline when fielded on the glove side.

(a)   (b)

(c)   (d)

worse by overreacting in panic fashion. It is imperative to make a clean
pickup on the first try and then release a strong and accurate throw to the
relay man. Bobbles or off-target throws can add even more bases to those
already assured the baserunner(s). He must realize that while it certainly
is not his fault that this long drive has been hit, he could indeed be the

cause of further problems. Neither panic nor faulty body control should be allowed to result in a bobble or poor throw. Good technique in getting to and rid of the ball may still contribute to a putout on the bases. That would result in an outfield assist. Leading the team in outfield assists is a prized plum that every outfielder should want to earn. Producing more assists than errors is yet another desirable statistic for the outfielder.

With a drive to or off the fence, the outfielder should be wary of improper body positioning at the time of the pickup as well as the chance of taking his eye off the ball during the pickup. The position of the feet with respect to the target will greatly influence the accuracy and speed of release. For that reason, proper procedure for playing the rebound must become second nature through practice. As mentioned in the chapter on positioning, the outfielder must understand what to expect from the ball's impact with the fence or wall. Whether the rebound will consist of a vertical thud or a lively kickback is something that must be determined beforehand through study and experimentation.

Some balls may be tracked down toward the throwing-arm side while others will cause the outfielder to move toward his glove side as he approaches the rebounding ball. In studying the procedures for each, assume the outfielder to be right-handed.

First, consider the ball rebounding to his throwing-arm side. The key to a clean pickup on the first try is a step with the right foot *beyond* the ball. As he begins to bend in the knees and waist to begin his barehanded pickup, the ball must be directly beneath him, not beyond his right foot. This way, his eyes are less apt to be taken off the ball, since it is centered in front of and between his feet. Then, the pickup is followed by the outfielder's choice of crowhop to produce good body balance as well as forward momentum toward the awaiting target of the middle infielder. The arm must be kept up and the elbow high to produce the strongest overhand throw possible.

As a right-handed outfielder makes the pickup, he finds that he has actually executed a reverse pivot, having turned 180 degrees in a counterclockwise direction toward the player's glove side (Photo Series 8-5).

The rebound to the glove-hand side is handled similarly (Photo Series 8-6). Again, he takes a step not to the ball, but beyond it. In this straddle position, he is situated perfectly for a one-handed, barehanded pickup. Despite the one-handed pickup, the glove is still positioned down and next to the ball to help keep the head down and eyes on the ball.

It can't be stressed enough that he must step past the ball. Otherwise, he will find himself reaching back beyond his right foot. Doing this will often move the eyes off the ball, resulting in a bobble.

The crowhop then begins. In making any throw following a reverse pivot, the temptation is to allow the throwing-side elbow to droop. While the ball may be released quicker this way, the throw will lack the directly

PHOTO SERIES 8-5: Fielding the Ball Off the Fence to the Throwing-Arm Side

To pick up the ball and get rid of it as quickly as possible, the outfielder uses a reverse pivot. He steps beyond the ball to be able to field it directly in front of him and between the legs.

(a)

(b)

(c)

Photo Series 8-5 (cont'd)

(d)

overhand motion needed for maximum carry. In addition, throughout that quick crowhop, the line through the shoulders must be riveted on the target to assure that the upper body has closed as the arm is extended back. To do otherwise will cause the ball to sail and will again take something off it.

PHOTO SERIES 8-6: Fielding the Ball Off the Fence to the Glove Side
This pickup does not require any reverse pivot but merely a straddle of the ball. A common mistake outfielders make is to reach back for the ball instead of reaching straight down from a straddle position.

(a)

(b)

DRILLS AND METHODS OF INSTRUCTION

With every hit that makes its way to an outfielder, the coach hopes to see three objectives met in the fielding and follow-up throw.

First, he looks for quickness and efficiency in getting to the ball. This involves (1) a good break, (2) charging and/or rounding the ball as needed, and (3) using the most advantageous fielding method, given the field condition and game situation.

Second, the coach hopes to see the most prudent decision possible made on the outfielder's intended throwing target. This part is all mental. It is the strategy employed by the outfielder based on his knowledge of the many factors that contribute to this decision. It is something he should have been planning even prior to the ball being hit. Making such correct throwing decisions and targets is our center of attention in Chapter 9.

Third is the footwork (crowhop) following the catch and the throw itself. The coach hopes to see his outfielder get off a strong and accurate throw. This is the only objective that has already been discussed in an earlier chapter with accompanying drills as well.

Note that the third objective, along with the first, deals with technique while the second objective is purely strategic in nature. Until you are satisfied with the techniques being used by your outfielders, it is best to avoid this second objective in selecting drills dealing with fielding hits and making follow-up throws. To drill strategy assumes good technique already exists. In any such drill, be careful to avoid making the outfielder work on his techniques and strategy simultaneously. The outfielder can't be expected to concentrate on improving some physical aspect of fielding a base hit while simultaneously trying to decide his most strategic target. In a game, the outfielder's thinking process must be concerned with the throwing strategy, which is always changing with the runner situation and those many factors already discussed. His mechanics in fielding the ball, however, must become second nature. For that reason, the drills used here dwell on technique and present a no-doubt-about-it target for the outfielder's throw. In Chapter 9, the emphasis of the drills shifts to throwing strategy. That will take place only after the full gamut of throwing strategy is discussed in that chapter.

Drills: Fielding the Hits

Unless a large, fieldhouse type of facility is available, any indoor work is best broken down into either (1) the approach and fielding of the ball or (2) the follow-up crowhop, release, and follow-through. In a smaller gym, then, hit or throw ground balls from one far end of the gym toward the other. To really get the feel for charging or rounding a ground ball base hit, the players, taking turns while lined up at the other end, should be given about one-half the length of the gym for this purpose. Of course, the balls can't be hit or thrown very hard or fast if the players are to have enough time and room to practice their charging or rounding.

To drill this base hit fielding technique, the coach may wish to face the wall at his end and hurl an indoor type of ball at it, sometimes at a slight angle to his left or right. This will vary the kickback angle and will keep the outfielders "honest" down at the other end. This way, they will be less able to predetermine the direction of the base hit. Again, though, the rebound can't be made to come off the wall too hard or the outfielder will have little time to practice his approach to the ball. The coach may either restrict the drill to the usual infielders' method of going down for the ball or work instead on the do-or-die side-scoop method or the one-knee-drop variation. However, the coach must be sure to keep the base hits low to the ground for the one-knee-drop method.

As soon as each ball enters the glove, the outfielder freezes, thus allowing both his coach as well as himself a chance to study his positioning and make any suggestions or corrections. No follow-up throws are made. Instead, the ball is rolled back to the coach or to the individual catching for him (Diagram 8-1).

A more basic and elementary "rounding" fielding drill can be run without a ball being hit. To begin, six outfielders are spaced ten feet apart against the gym wall at one end. Six balls are likewise placed ten feet apart along the centerline (widthwise) of the gym. Then, as each outfielder takes his turn, the coach points to the ball that he wants charged, rounded, and fielded. The outfielder will have half the gym to execute the movement. Depending on the position of the outfielder and the position of the ball approached, the outfielder may be required to perform a lot of rounding. Then, again, he may be asked to charge a ball directly in front of him. At contact with the ball, the outfielder will again freeze for his coach's scrutiny before replacing the ball in its original place and returning to the gym wall for his next charge. In returning, the outfielder takes up that position directly in line with the ball he just fielded. This way, he will have greater opportunity to round balls both to his left and right. As the drill continues, the coach attempts to supply a number of differently angled balls for each outfielder to approach and field (Diagram 8-2).

Drills: The Follow-up Throws

With limited space and now wishing to drill the crowhop and throw phase of the base hit, the coach may try this drill. Have each outfielder in turn begin by placing a "dead" ball on the floor about ten feet in front of him. Each outfielder then backs up ten feet to the gym wall. Although he

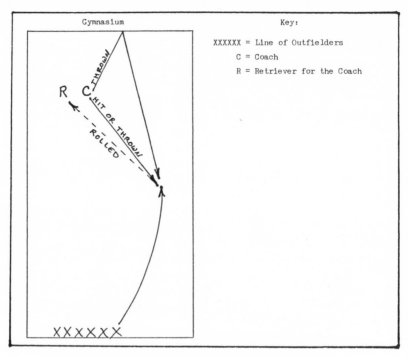

DIAGRAM 8-1:   Indoor "Base Hit" Fielding Drill
The coach has the option of either rebounding the ball off the wall or
hitting or throwing it directly toward the outfielder.

won't have room to charge or round the hit, he will be able to descend into
his fielding position, make the pickup, crowhop, throw, and follow-
through. Three infielders are used as targets to receive the throws at the
other end of the gym. This way, sufficient space should allow for almost a
gym-length throw. With the entire gym floor available and working with
six outfielders, three stations can be set up, each using one-third of the
gym floor. Each station will find two outfielders alternating at one end and
their targeted infielder at the other (Diagram 8-3). The infielders then
return the balls to the outfielders who threw them, while the other
outfielders are setting up the balls for their turns.

In place of infielders receiving the throws, the coach may wish to tape
targets on the far end wall of the gym for each of the three stations. Each
target must be at least six feet up the wall. However, unless room allows
for throws of at least 100 feet, such accuracy testing is best left for the
outdoors.

The coach, trying his best to scrutinize all three stations, may allow

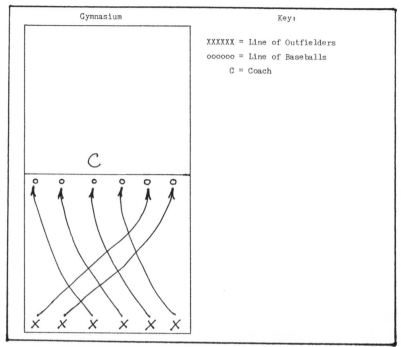

DIAGRAM 8-2: Indoor "Rounding" Fielding Drill
No balls are picked up or thrown as the outfielders make their approaches one at a time. The coach can use any of dozens of possible routes for the six outfielders.

each outfielder his own choice of crowhop or may insist on one particular type. This type of experimentation may help each outfielder discover not only the techniques used in each crowhop, but their unique advantages and disadvantages as well. By drill's end, each outfielder will hopefully have found a home with the crowhop method that provides him the most efficient and comfortable release.

Unfortunately, the above drill cannot measure accuracy very well. Outdoors, though, this two-part drill can be combined into one. Utilizing the full expanse of the outfield, the placement of the coach's fungo hits, and using any one of three base targets, all of the ingredients studied and drilled indoors will come together. Each outfielder still has a definite pre-set target, so he can concentrate on technique, technique, and more technique! The strategy of deciding which base to throw to will come in later drills once these fielding and throwing techniques have become more fully developed.

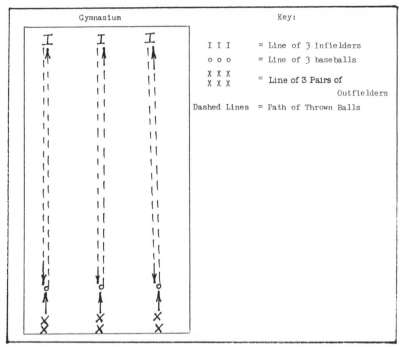

DIAGRAM 8-3:   Indoor "Pickup, Crowhop, and Throw" Drill
Each outfielder, upon making a throw, then awaits the return throw from
the infielder. He then resets the ball for the next outfielder at his station.

Drills: The Balls Hit Down the Line and Into the Gaps

For balls hit down the line or into the gaps, the gym provides only
limited practice opportunities. This type of hit requires much rounding
and sometimes the use of the reverse pivot. Both of these techniques can
be simulated indoors, but it isn't until the players are outdoors that they
can practice "airing out" their arms with strong, hard throws, usually
toward second base.

The regular field with the outfielders stationed at their respective
positions and the fungo-wielding coach at home provides the best setting
from which to practice these skills. Center fielders are not needed if only
the foul lines are going to be worked, but to keep all the outfielders
working and honest, too, the coach will usually want to include work on
gappers as well as balls hit down the line. This will prevent the left and
right fielders from shading toward the lines. The coach then divides his
hits between the two foul lines and the two gap areas. All throws are
directed toward second base, using the other middle infielder as a relay

man where necessary. On any ball where the outfielder refuses to concede a double, his low, hard throw should ideally reach the base on one big hop.

Just when the players are really beginning to get a feel for this play, it comes time to throw in a more realistic dimension... a runner.

Using several non-outfielders as runners, the coach has each runner attempt a double as he belts out the "maybe" extra-base hit. Knowing that every runner will be trying for two bases will keep the outfielders hustling after every ball, certainly more so than without their use. The offense and defense may wish to keep score against each other. The defense will soon learn that with hustle, good and efficient technique, and a strong, accurate throw, a lot of runners will end up on the short end of the call at second base. Such results will go a long way toward producing an outfield of confidence and character.

Drills: The Extra-Base Hits to the Fence or Off the Wall

Practice next those extra-base hits that travel to or rebound off a wall or fence. Pitchers must be made to understand that such drills are inserted not in any way to demean the staff or cast a pessimistic outlook on the season, but rather to bolster the staff's confidence in their outfielders. When those occasional deep drives are hit, a good outfielder will make the batter and any runners earn every base they get. What's well deserved, fine, but not a base more! And, who knows? Perhaps in the process, an overly aggressive or foolhardy runner can be thrown out as a result of an efficient pickup and a solid throw.

When playing on the road, every outfielder should be reminded to check out the "bounceability" of any wall or fence, along with any openings or other unique characteristics. That goes double for his own home park, where any such drills will take place.

One good indoor drill for this purpose is called, "Fido, fetch!" Needed are the coach, all the team's outfielders, and one infielder to handle the throws. All stand at one end of the gym with the infielder next to the coach and the line of outfielders a few feet away but still against the wall. The coach then throws or fungoes a ball across the length of the gym against the opposite wall. Sometimes, he will hit the wall on a fly and other times on a bounce or roll. Occasionally, he will hit it so softly that the ball won't even reach the opposite wall. As the ball is hit or thrown, the outfielder whose turn it is runs almost the full length of the gym floor, retrieving the ball as efficiently as possible. Usually, it will be retrieved as it rebounds off the wall, but sometimes it will be tracked down before it even reaches the wall. As the ball is picked up, the outfielder wheels to his glove-hand side as he crowhops and attempts to throw a perfect relay back to the waiting infielder. The running involved makes this drill a fine

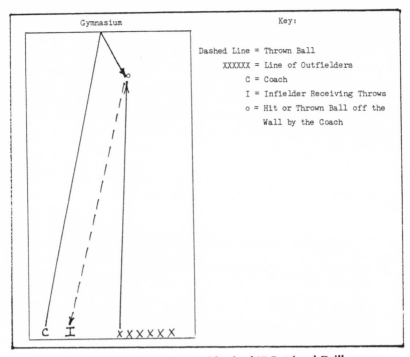

DIAGRAM 8-4:   Indoor "Fido, fetch!" Retrieval Drill
The coach may wish to flip-flop his own position with that of his
outfielders. This would force the right-handed outfielders to retrieve
most of the balls off their throwing-arm side, requiring the use of the
reverse pivot.

conditioner, too. The mechanics of the placement of the body over the ball
along with proper crowhop and throwing-action techniques are closely
scrutinized by the coach (Diagram 8-4).

Outdoors, the coach may work the same drill by fungoing the ball
from the infield grass in the vicinity of second base. Each of the three
outfielders is told to take a shallow position to allow most of the coach's
hits to make their way to the fence or wall. Two middle infielders rotate as
the relay man in the short outfield grass. That infielder then relays to the
other at second base, who then flips it back to the coach for his next hit. The
aggressive outfielder will often try to good-naturedly spoil the coach's
intent by catching the ball on a fly or, in whatever manner, just not letting
the ball get past him. The hits are rotated to all three outfielders.

A variation of the above drill has the three outfielders each being
assigned his own relay man. Each relay man is given a ball to begin the
drill. Therefore, with three balls being used simultaneously, the relay men
can then throw each "a drive to the fence or off the wall." Each outfielder

then hustles to retrieve the ball as he would in a game. The relay is made to the outfielder's personal relay man. Relay throws are then made to infielders awaiting the throws at second base and third base or to the catcher at home. The left fielder's relay man throws to third base, while the relay man in short-center throws to second base. The relay man in short-right throws home. This way, as a safety measure, no balls find themselves criss-crossing on their way to a base (Diagram 8-5).

If other drills are taking place in the infield, the coach may elect to have the three relay men just wheel and fake throws to the bases. At that point, they would begin anew with another toss to the fence to begin a new play.

Another indoor drill can also be used for this purpose. Working in pairs, each outfielder and his partner (another outfielder) face each other from opposite ends of the gym floor but with their backs twenty feet from the wall behind them. One ball is used for each pair. The outfielder with the ball gets down somewhat similar to a center in football and "hikes" or rolls the ball back those twenty feet so the ball will rebound off the wall

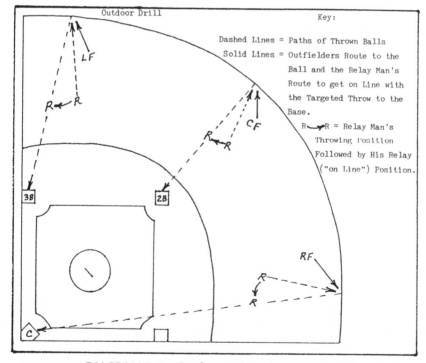

DIAGRAM 8-5:   Outdoor "Hit to the Fence" Drill
This drill variation allows the coach greater time to critique since the relay men are the ones sending the balls to the fence. No fungo bats are used.

behind him. He immediately gives chase back to the ball. Again, using hustle and proper fielding technique, he throws to his partner-outfielder, who serves as the relay man. Then, upon receiving the throw, this second outfielder similarly continues the drill by hiking the ball back to his wall. If the whole gym is available, it should easily accommodate three pairs of outfielders. This routine is known as the "Off-the-Wall" Fielding Drill (Diagram 8-6).

This next outdoor drill is known as the "5-Ball Successive Pickup and Throw" Drill. The outfielder places five balls ten feet apart on a diagonal line back toward the fence. The diagonal line of balls may extend either left or right as the outfielder faces the fence. One infielder is needed as a relay man to receive the throws of the outfielder. After placing the five balls, the outfielder assumes his normal depth position. Again, the idea is to simulate the chasing-down of the long drive. To begin, he drop steps and sprints to the nearest ball. Stepping over the ball, he makes the pickup, crowhops, and throws. From there, he quickly hurries to each of the next four balls in succession. Similarly, he attempts to make an efficient

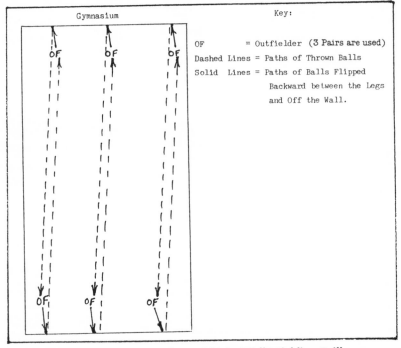

DIAGRAM 8-6:   Indoor "Off-the-Wall" Fielding Drill
As many as six outfielders can work simultaneously here on their retrieval
techniques and throwing mechanics.

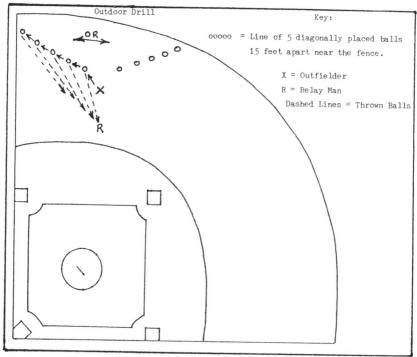

DIAGRAM 8-7: "5-Ball Successive Pickup and Throw" Drill
For the right-handed outfielder, the chase to the five balls lined up to his left side (not pictured) will require the use of a reverse pivot for each pickup. A larger gym or fieldhouse could accommodate this drill indoors as well.

crowhop and accurate throw. The awaiting relay man stations himself 150 feet away or somewhat less for lower levels. If desired, the relay man may be another outfielder, in which case the two of them can alternate and compete with each other as well. The accuracy of the throws may then translate into a friendly scoring system. Award 2 points for a perfect pickup and throw and 1 point for an acceptable, but non-perfect throw. No points are awarded a poor pickup or throw. This way, picking up the ball cleanly and hitting the target soon become a habit (Diagram 8-7).

Drills: Throwing Strength and Accuracy

A drill that tests for throwing strength and accuracy involves a long throw into the plate from center field. Used outdoors, it is simply and appropriately known as the "Throwing Strength and Accuracy" Drill. From a marked-off line 260 feet from the plate (again, much less for the lower levels), the drill begins. Using a stopwatch, the coach times and

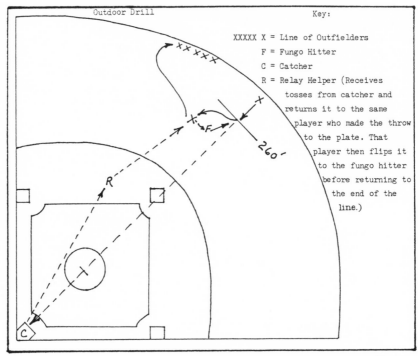

Outdoor Drill

Key:

XXXXX X = Line of Outfielders

F = Fungo Hitter

C = Catcher

R = Relay Helper (Receives tosses from catcher and returns it to the same player who made the throw to the plate. That player then flips it to the fungo hitter before returning to the end of the line.)

DIAGRAM 8-8:   Outdoor "Throwing Strength and Accuracy" Drill
The ground ball fungo hit by the coach need not travel far. As the ball is hit, the outfielder moves in on the ball as he would with any base hit.

grades for accuracy as the outfielders take turns throwing to the plate. Each outfielder begins behind this line as a ball is rolled or hit his way from a short distance of about 100 feet. Ideally, the outfielder would like to throw the ball on a line and have it arrive at the plate on one bounce. The timing would measure glove-to-glove contact; that is, from the moment the ball first contacts the outfielder's glove until it touches the catcher's mitt. Accuracy is determined by whether or not the catcher receives the ball in contact with or straddling the plate. No relay man is used. Often used by scouts at tryout camps, this drill can also help the coach evaluate the arms of his outfielders. Special care must be taken that the outfielders be especially loose and warmed up sufficiently because of the long throws involved. For the same reason, the number of throws made by each outfielder should not exceed about ten (Diagram 8-8).

If eight outfielders are available, they can form two four-member teams for a "Throwing-Relay Race" Drill. Held in the expanse of the outfield, the two teams prepare by forming two long parallel lines. Members of each team are about 150 feet from each other with their two "end" members about 600 feet apart. The same end man for each team is given a ball. The coach may ask for a normal "one end to the other and back again" routing of the ball or may wish to devise a more unique circuit of throws. Anytime a team drops a ball, it immediately loses that heat. Players soon learn the importance of concentration in the execution of their throwing mechanics. A predetermined number of heat victories determines the winning team in this spirited drill.

Because outfielders need drill in their pickups and initial throws as opposed to relays, asking each receiver of a throw to intentionally drop the throw, pick it up again, and throw is a variation of the above relay drill. With the exception of the very last catch, then, every other catch is quickly dropped and recovered as quickly as possible and followed by a crowhop and snappy throw (Diagram 8-9).

A less rigorous or complicated drill involves two outfielders playing catch from about 260 feet apart (or less for the lower levels). The only

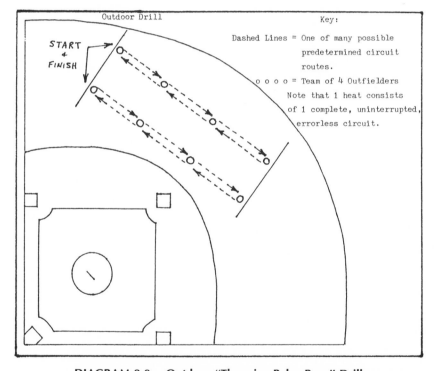

DIAGRAM 8-9:   Outdoor "Throwing-Relay Race" Drill

An appealing feature here is the vast variety of routes that can be devised. In addition, pickup and crowhop techniques can be incorporated by requiring that each throw be dropped and then quickly recovered (except by the last man of the circuit).

difference is that each player tries to "one bounce" the ball in to his partner as he would when throwing directly to a base. Of course, a crowhop precedes the throw, and the single bounce should ideally be a big one. Dirt is preferred as the surface for the bounces, since the ball may have a tendency to skid somewhat on grass. In reality, dirt will be the surface substance on throws to the bases, while grass will serve likewise on throws to the plate.

Chapter 9

Strategies to Stop Advancing Runners

INTRODUCTION

Sometimes outfielders feel or are made to feel that their position holds little strategy. With our early discussions of positional strategy in Chapters 3 and 4, that notion has hopefully come to an end. Recall that the first strategy studied involved the question, "Where can I best position myself for this batter as he comes to the plate?"

The second positioning strategy studied tried to answer the question, "How should I change my positioning for a given batter since each pitch changes his count for the better or worse?"

Third, backup roles and responsibilities were covered to answer this important question, "How can I best help my team when a play is being made on a runner or when the ball is hit to someone other than myself?"

Now that fly ball and base hit fielding and throwing mechanics have been thoroughly examined and analyzed, it comes time to study two final types of outfield strategy. Both are closely related as they attempt to answer our last, but very crucial question of outfield strategy. The question is this: "Now that I have just caught a fly ball or have fielded a hit, to which base should I throw the ball and why?" Of course, the more runners on base at the time, the tougher the necessary decisions. However, we will learn that even with no runners on base, there are certain strategic throwing guidelines to follow.

Let's begin with a look at the throwing strategies surrounding the catch of a fly ball with one or more runners on base with less than two outs. This is known as the fly-ball/tag-up play and, unless the throwing distance is prohibitive, it offers the outfielder the opportunity to go one-on-one against an advancing runner. If victorious, the reward is a prized assist and, perhaps, the key to saving a ball game.

DEFENSING THE FLY-BALL/TAG-UP PLAY:
SINGLE-RUNNER SITUATIONS

Most throwing strategy for outfielders involves situations following the fielding of hits. However, there are also a number of strategic situations involving fly balls caught with one or more runners on base. With multiple runners on base, the outfielder must already have in mind the base to which he will target his throw.

Given a particular situation, one might define strategies as "reactions of choice." The most beneficial reaction choice is dependent upon several factors. These variables include the number of outs, the number and position of the runners, the score, inning, and knowledge of the speed of the runners. Not to be forgotten is the outfielder's realistic understanding of his arm's capabilities. This is what game involvement and anticipation is all about. Such thinking must continue to take place between pitches, and when it does, will pay handsome dividends. Certainly it is one of the characteristics that distinguish the great outfielder from the mediocre one. The average outfielder thinks, too, but not as intensely and continuously as does the outstanding one. Occasionally, mental lapses may actually cause the mediocre outfielder to formulate his strategic response *after* catching the ball, often demonstrating this unpreparedness with a marked hesitation in releasing the ball. Sometimes, too, inexperience or lack of sufficient forethought will cause his chosen response to be one of the poorer strategic choices.

In determining the course of action to a given situation, all of the above-mentioned factors must be funneled down into two prime considerations.

First, what is the safest base to which the ball may be thrown to halt the runner's advances? By "safest" is meant the base that is ninety feet beyond the lead runner at the time of the pickup.

Second, does the depth of the fly, arm strength, score, inning, and importance of the runner(s) suggest that the throw go toward some base other than the safest? This second consideration also implies a more important question. Might it be more prudent at times to discourage or halt the advance of a back runner than to challenge a runner trying to advance home from third? Let's examine each of these possible tag-up situations.

Tag-Up Strategy: Runner at Third Base

With a lone runner on third and less than two outs, the outfielder should get rid of the ball immediately with a strong throw to the plate. Whether the ball comes into the catcher on one bounce or a fly doesn't matter. It is rare when enough time exists for the relay man to successfully relay an off-target throw to the catcher for a putout. All that matters is whether the throw will beat the runner.

A rare but noteworthy exception to that rule may occur in the bottom half of the last or extra innings when the runner on third represents the winning run. If the fly ball is catchable, but definitely foul, he should let it drop rather than see the winning run cross the plate. Only if the fly ball is so shallow that chances are good of holding the runner at third or throwing him out at the plate should the catch and follow-up throw be made.

Tag-Up Strategy: Runner at Second Base or First Base

With a single runner on second or first, the obvious throw would be to the next base, with care being taken not to get suckered by the runner. The runner may dart off his base, but then stop, hoping to advance to the next base when the unsuspecting outfielder throws behind the runner instead of to the base in front of him.

DEFENSING THE TAG-UP PLAY: MULTIPLE-RUNNER SITUATIONS

With runners on second and third, should the throw go home or to third? With runners on first and third, should the throw go home or to second? With runners on first and second, should the throw go to third or to second? And, of course, with the bases loaded, should the throw go home, to third, or to second?

Responses to all these situations must be determined within the framework of the two considerations mentioned earlier. Again, those two considerations are: (1) What is the safest base to which the ball should be thrown to halt runner advances? and (2) Does the depth of the fly, the outfielder's arm strength, score, inning, and importance of the runners suggest that the throw go toward some base other than the safest? In some cases this would allow a runner to advance home unchallenged.

If no factor is found in this second consideration to be prohibitive to throwing to that base beyond the lead runner, then that's where the throw should go. However, because so often there is a glaring drawback to this strategy, a throw to another base becomes the smarter choice.

Tag-Up Strategy: Runners at Second and Third

With runners at second and third, for example, it might seem that the throw should go home after the catch. Yes, he should throw home if it represents the winning run. Further, if the outfielder senses that a good chance exists of getting the man at the plate after considering the fly ball's depth, the runner's speed, and his own arm strength, then he should also throw home. However, if any of these factors suggests otherwise, then the throw should be to third base to hold the runner at second base. In these 50-50 toss-up situations, the outfielder must be guided by the answer to this question, "Will giving the opposition a run here, considering the inning and score, greatly affect our team's chances to win?"

Tag-Up Strategy: Runners at First and Third

Similar logic is used in this first and third situation. If he decides not to throw home, then he should throw into second base. This will preserve the double-play possibility with the next hitter by discouraging the advance of the runner at first. It is sometimes better to prevent a runner from advancing to third or getting into scoring position at second, even if a throw there allows the lead runner to score. One consideration is the small percentage of outfield throws to the plate that get their man. Nothing short of perfect execution will produce the out at the plate.

Tag-Up Strategy: Runners at First and Second

With runners at first and second, it would seem that the safe and smart throw would go to third. However, a throw to second might be even smarter if the fly is deep to center or right field. This especially would be the case with a very fast runner at second base. Even without an exceptionally fast runner at second, a fly ball caught in deep right field would best be directed to second base.

Tag-Up Strategy: Runners at First, Second, and Third

In a bases-loaded situation, the throw home is in order if the runner at third is the winning run or if you believe the odds are good of getting the man there. If that is not the case, then the guidelines mentioned above for runners on first and second should apply.

Tag-Up Strategy: Conclusion

In general, with a comfortable lead, the defense can afford to give up the run and opt to concentrate on a backrunner. When behind, especially in the later stages of the game, the outfielder may want to "go for broke" and try for the perfect execution needed to get the man at the plate. Being put one more run behind at this point, though, could spell gloom, unless the team has an explosive offense.

So you can see, then, that there are few pat answers to any of these multiple-runner situations, only guidelines. These guidelines also demonstrate to the outfielder the importance of mulling over the advantages and disadvantages of his options should a fly ball come his way. Even then, his preplanned strategy may have to be scrapped due to the depth of the fly ball. All the while, too, he must continue to reposition himself as the count and other facts change.

This discussion of tag-up strategy might best be concluded with a quote. Former standout Yankee outfielder, Tommy Henrich, may have said it best when he stated, "Catching a fly ball is a pleasure, but knowing what to do with it after you catch it is a business."

THROWING STRATEGIES TO DEFENSE THE HIT:
SINGLE-RUNNER SITUATIONS

Outside of some efficient positioning, there isn't much the outfielder can do to stop a batter from getting a hit. That task falls on the shoulders of the battery. But while he may not be able to defense the hit itself, his follow-up throw can stop an advancing runner in his tracks. With one or more runners on base, the follow-up throw takes on an importance every bit as crucial as those following fly ball catches.

The runner or runners are already on the move, but how bold and aggressive— or foolhardy—will they become? Will they try to take the extra base, and if they do, can the outfielder make it one base too many for them? To get that runner, he must not only make an accurate and strong throw, but he must begin by correctly deciding which base to throw to. Even with just one runner on base at the time of a hit, there are two possible targets. With two or three runners, the number of choices is even greater. The factors that go into these kinds of decisions along with other throwing guidelines, including some with no runners on base, comprise the throwing strategy studied here.

A single runner on base will provide a choice between attempting to stop the advance of the lead runner or limiting the advance of the batter-runner. Of course, in many instances there will be no other runners on base. It might seem, then, that with only the batter-runner to contend with, throwing strategy might be nonexistent. However, there do exist some general guidelines and throwing principles to consider. These should be followed upon the fielding of every hit.

Throwing Strategy: No Runners on Base

Most important is getting the ball back into the infield as quickly and efficiently as possible. The ball should always be played as if the runner might attempt to take an extra base. This way, the outfielder will be sure to get rid of the ball quickly and not hold onto it; he should never dare the runner to take an extra base by holding the ball.

Occasionally, though, on a hit to right field, the runner may carelessly round first base a bit too aggressively. In this case, the outfielder can demonstrate his own defensive aggressiveness by attempting to pick off such a runner by throwing behind him. The throw is made to either the first baseman or to the catcher covering the base. The outfielder must be convinced, though, that the runner is not actually lulling him into a throw that will find the runner breaking for second base rather than back to first as soon as the ball is thrown. The usual strategy, with no one on base, is to throw ahead of the runner to prevent any further advance.

The outfielder uses all his fielding opportunities and not just his pregame throws to show off his arm to the opposition. Even without any runner trying to advance, all throws should be made hard and low with the throwing-arm elbow held high. Even short throws should be made overhand and thrown off the proper foot. Every such throw will help provide a psychological edge, demonstrating not only a strong arm, but a strong desire and commitment, too.

On a routine base hit, the throw is targeted to the middle infielder near second base. The middle infielder closest to the outfielder will set up as the cut man. A good throw should be shoulder to chest high as it comes in to the cut man. He will cut it off if the runner isn't coming or if the throw is off the mark. He'll know when the throw is off the mark since the position he'll take to receive the possible cut will be in line between the targeted base and the outfielder.

If the runner does try to advance to second base, any strong and accurate throw will not be cut off. Instead, the cut man will allow the throw to continue to the base where it should ideally arrive on one big bounce. A shorter throw may arrive on a fly without a bounce but must remain low enough to be cut off when off the mark.

When the throw is coming from the left fielder, the right fielder moves in to help in case of any overthrow. The left fielder reciprocates when the throw is coming into second base from the right fielder.

With no one on base, the extra-base hit requires virtually no strategic decisions. The relay man and his trailer (the nearest and next-nearest middle infielders, respectively) are the ones doing the thinking. If the relay man feels the throw should be made to third base, for example, then he will align himself with that base. On the other hand, if he feels the batter has a sure three-bagger but may try for an inside-the-park round tripper, the relay man will instead set up in a line between home plate and the outfielder. In either case, his hands will be high above his head to facilitate a quick sighting of him. This is especially important when the outfielder must turn his back to the infield to chase down a long drive or to retrieve a shot off the fence. When he does make the pickup and turns to throw, he must be able to immediately spot the waving arms of the relay man.

Sometimes, an extra-base hit will roll under an outfield fence. Never should the ball be retrieved by reaching under the fence. Instead, the outfielder should raise both arms before turning back toward the infield to indicate to the umpires that the ball has rolled into dead ball area. As soon as the umpire has verified the ball's location, he will award the batter two bases as set down in almost all ground rules. After all, what outfielder shouldn't be thrilled with holding a batter to a double when the latter's drive rolls all the way to the fence and under it?

When playing a straightaway position in either left or right field, he should accept the fact that balls hit down the foul lines or very close to them will result in sure doubles. Care should be taken not to overrun the ball in panic, thus playing it into a triple. This is especially true in right field where a bobble of any sort on a ball hit down the line will surely send the runner on to third base. Because of the long throw involved and the likelihood of the runner arriving safely, discretion tells the right fielder to concede the double and go all out to corral the ball under control without a mishap.

Throwing Strategy: Runner at First Base

Next to having no runners on base, the next most commonly faced situation is that of the sole runner at first base. As common as this situation may be, however, the outfielder suddenly finds himself having to decide between two possible targets for the upcoming throw. Which runner should he pursue, the lead runner or the hitter? To make a prudent choice, he must think about this beforehand to be able to get rid of the ball quickly without "double-clutching." Some of this decision making, though, can only be made after the ball has been hit, since the nature and direction of the hit itself are big factors in the decision process. Another consideration is that the relay man can only line himself up with one base, and sometimes that base may not be the most strategic one to throw to.

Again, the outfielder considers many factors when preparing for a possible hit to come his way with that runner on first base. He considers the inning, the score, the importance and position of the runner (at the moment the hit is fielded), the runner's speed, the number of outs, and his own throwing strength as well. He realizes, too, that the ideal target base may have to be altered due to the type of base hit. It may be hit hard and straight at him, a few or many steps to one side or the other, softly hit in front of him, or even over his head.

In a close game, the outfielder tries to keep any tying or winning run out of scoring position. Often, that may mean conceding the advance of the lead runner to third base to hold the hitter to first base.

When it's not crucial that the hitter be kept out of scoring position, he targets the throw to third base. It doesn't matter whether the runner from first has made an all-out attempt to advance there or whether he is just beginning to round the bag at second. Only if no chance exists to stop the advancing runner from reaching third should the throw go into second base. In throwing to third, the outfielder locates the shortstop with upraised arms in line between the target base and himself. The relay man will try to set up at a distance from third base that will allow the throw to reach him chest high. That way, he can cut off a late or off-the-mark throw. Also, he might cut the throw and relay to second base in an attempt to retire the batter-runner trying to advance there. The shortstop, always wishing to receive the throw chest high, will learn through experience to vary his distance from the base depending on the arm strength of the outfielder making the throw.

As the ball is fielded, the outfielder is guided by the position of the lead runner at that instant. To have a play at third, he spots the advancing runner no more than two strides past second, except occasionally in the case of the left fielder whose throwing distance is so much shorter. Otherwise, a throw to second is the smarter move. Not only will it keep the hitter from moving into scoring position, but it will also leave open the chance for a double play with the next hitter whenever there are less than two outs. Usually, if the base hit is softly hit, bobbled, or hit in a direction away from the outfielder, the more prudent throw is to second base.

With a runner on first and less than two outs, he can sometimes "con" the runner into thinking that a short fly ball is going to hang up long enough to be caught. As he races in for this short, quickly sinking fly ball that he has no chance of reaching, the outfielder raises his hands as if preparing to make the catch. The runner from first will often slow up to see if the ball will be caught. Sometimes, he may even stop in the basepath. When conned this way, the runner will find himself advancing no further than second and, occasionally, will even be forced out on the play. The same play can be worked with just about any other single- or multiple-runner situation.

Throwing Strategy: Runner at Second Base

The single to the outfield with a runner on second makes for one of the most exciting plays in baseball, as the runner on second matches the speed in his legs against the strength and accuracy of the outfielder's arm. As the runner begins his advance, the outfielder directs the throw toward the cut man who will have set up in the line of the throw to the plate. Usually, that assignment will go to the third baseman for throws from the left fielder (the shortstop will cover third) and to the first baseman for throws from the center fielder or from the right fielder. An attempt to get the ball all the way to the catcher on a fly should never be made unless this is the winning run trying to score in the last inning. The throw must be low enough to be handled by the cut man who will usually set up about 70 feet from the plate.

If there is no chance of the throw beating the runner to the plate, it should go instead to second base. Again, that decision should be based on the position of the runner rounding third as well as on the strength of the outfielder's own arm and the distance to the plate. With the runner more than two strides past third, the throw is best targeted to second base. This is also the wisest target when holding a comfortable lead. This guideline works especially well for the right fielder and also the center fielder since the baseline can be seen along with the runner. The distance of the runner past third can be more easily judged this way.

On the other hand, the left fielder must often make his throw without clear sight of the baseline. Even if the baseline is in view, the decision to throw home or to second isn't made any easier since the baseline, the runner, and the throw home are all on near-parallel paths. For this reason, a left fielder unfortunately stands the best chance of the three outfielders of seeing his throw hit the runner.

When throwing home, he tries to make the ball arrive on one big hop, not on a fly. This is perhaps the outfielder's greatest opportunity for an assist. One goal of every outfielder should be to chalk up more assists than errors during the season. Good technique coupled with plenty of concentration when going down for the pickups can make that goal a reality. A lack of concentration will so often result in a bobble. Only excellent mechanics including a great follow-through will produce a strong and on-target throw.

Throwing Strategy: Runner at Third Base

The sole runner on third will obviously score on any single to the outfield. Therefore, the outfielder coming up with the ball following a hit need only concern himself with the batter-runner as he would with no one on base.

Single-Runner Throwing-Strategy Guidelines

Exceptions will always exist, but in general, with a single runner at first or second, the hits that get to the outfielder can be categorized into one of these four groups, and the response should be as suggested.

1. The hard line-drive single hit directly at him will produce the greatest opportunity to throw out the advancing runner.

2. Many singles, both line drives and on the ground, require a lateral movement of several steps to get to the ball. With this type of base hit, the most prudent decision is to throw the ball in toward second base.

3. The softer, but direct single that requires a movement in for the ball is the one that will usually require the greatest judgment. He should be guided by the position of the lead runner just after the ball is fielded.

4. Finally, for almost all extra-base hits, he should target the relay man with his throw.

THROWING STRATEGIES: MULTIPLE-RUNNER SITUATIONS

Even with a single runner on base, the outfielder is faced with a multiple-runner situation. After all, the batter has instantly become a runner with his hit. Therefore, the choice to be made is between stopping the advance of the lead runner or holding the batter-runner to first base. However, there exist four possible multiple-runner situations prior to a pitch. These include: (1) runners on first and third, (2) runners on second and third, (3) runners on first and second, and (4) runners on first, second, and third.

Throwing Strategy: Runners at First and Third

The first and third as well as the second and third situations are the easiest multiple-runner situations to consider. It's a given, of course, that the runner on third will score easily on the hit. This allows for the first and third situation to be treated the same as that with a single runner at first base. The importance or non-importance of the run produced by the runner at third base should aid in the decision to throw to second or third base. The many other factors that lead to this decision have already been discussed earlier in this chapter.

Throwing Strategy: Runners at Second and Third

The situation of runners at second and third should be treated similarly to that of a single runner at second base. Again, the runner from third base will score easily. Ideally, the throw should go to the plate in a close game and to second base when holding a good lead. However, the factors contributing to this decision are many and have also been discussed. They are found in this chapter in the section dealing with the single runner at second base.

Throwing Strategy: Runners at First and Second or With the Bases Loaded

The first and second as well as the bases-loaded situation presents the same choices for the outfielder since, with the bases loaded, the runner from third base will score easily. In both cases, then, three choices present themselves. First, he may choose to throw home to stop the runner from second base. Second, he may throw to third base to put out or discourage the advance of the runner from first base. Finally, he may throw to second base to keep the batter-runner from moving up into scoring position.

With a nice lead, the defense would best forego any throw to the plate and concentrate, instead, on third base. This should occur if a throw there is advisable in view of the type of hit and the other factors that go into the decision. Otherwise, second base should become the target of the throw. Only in a close game should a throw to the plate take priority. In such close games, if the throw home seems a fruitless choice, then third base becomes the next best target.

DRILLS AND METHODS OF INSTRUCTION

Practicing techniques of outfield play such as catching various types of fly balls and fielding base hits can go just so far. Sooner or later, such drills must be combined with the strategies needed to combat different game situations involving runner advances.

Strategies surrounding the catch of a fly ball with less than two outs become more complex with the number of runners on base at the time. However, as long as even one runner is on base, a potential tag-up play is present. Overall, there is a total of seven possible single-, double-, and triple-runner situations, and you must prepare your players to deal strategically with all of them. They must be drilled not only on their techniques, but on their knowledge of where best to target their follow-up throws.

Even more complex are the throwing strategies following the fielding of a hit, where the batter, too, becomes an instant baserunner. Now, any of eight possible situations may face the outfielder.

The classroom may be a good starting point in which to explain the best possible responses to these fifteen total scenarios. However, the most tried and true format for drilling them, either one at a time or mixed, is out on the field. With the use of real runners and a full defense, outfielders are able to better perceive the situation and their available responses. With the help of the coach, the fungo bat, and runners, each of these fifteen single- or multiple-runner situations can be played out.

Some interesting variations of this basic drill pattern will be noted in the drills to follow. However, nothing can beat this method of instruction for providing each outfielder the opportunity to respond in a real way to each situation. The closer that such drills can be made to resemble a real game situation, the better. For that reason, too, the drills remain fun and retain the players' interest and enthusiasm.

Throwing-Strategy Drill

There is no trick to practicing the throwing strategies of the various single- and multiple-runner situations. There are four multiple-runner and four single-runner situations, if the batter with no one on base can be counted as one of the single-runner situations. To provide the needed perspective and reality of any of these eight situations, send a complete nine-man defense onto the field. All other players are used as helmeted runners. Drill just one of these situations at a time or mix and vary all eight of them.

Early in the season, it's usually best to begin with the more elementary single-runner situations, eventually finding time for all eight of the possible situations. Remember, though, that a hit with a runner on third presents the same throwing strategies that are present with no one on base. Hence, there are really just seven situations to cover. Working on one situation per practice session provides for a good and reasonable time schedule. As each of these is drilled, you may or may not wish to also include bunt defenses, double-play possibilities, and the like.

Once these seven individual practice sessions have provided the outfielders and defense in general with the experience and confidence needed, next mix the seven situations into future sessions. Mixing these situations while fungoing out the hits will keep the defense thinking. Only if the defense appears to begin having a definite problem with one of the seven situations might you decide to revert back to that lone situation for a more careful run-through.

Such "live runner" drills help the baserunning phase of the team's game as well. Runners are encouraged, though, to sometimes be a little overly aggressive to provide ample opportunities for the defense to make cuts in attempts to put out backrunners trying to advance.

All players must get rotated between offense and defense to emphasize the importance of each. This certainly includes the outfielders, who also need practice running the bases. In addition, this rotation will provide needed relief for the first group of baserunners and will give the defense a chance to use their brains and legs on the basepaths. All the while, constant advice and correction are given by the coach at home plate. As the coach belts out the hit off the fungo bat, the runner at home starts out from the batters' box. Any runners are asked to maintain conservative leadoffs. Sometimes, you may wish to drill these situations without a pitcher on the mound. With many of the hits directed toward center, this makes some sense for safety reasons. However, it's important, too, that pitchers learn to react quickly to hits by moving to appropriate backup positions. Furthermore, as stated earlier, the coach may decide to insert some infield plays. Some of these may include bunts or one-hoppers back to the mound, both of which involve the pitcher. When hitting from the plate area, then, it is wise for the coach to move a little away from the plate when hitting singles to center.

Finally, sliding is an important tool to consider in these drills. To slide or not to slide, that is the question! Certainly, safety must remain a strong consideration, but to what degree? Getting hit by a pitched ball probably presents the player with the greatest chance of injury, and yet we continue to provide live batting practice and live scrimmages. So why not sliding, too?

Sliding accomplishes several desirable objectives in this drill. First, it preserves the drill's necessary intensity. Second, sliding helps retain a semblance of reality in this make-believe situation. Finally, it presents some opportunities to practice the art of sliding.

For safety and comfort, first prepare the basepaths for comfortable and smooth slides through a thorough raking and grooming of each of the base areas.

Next, any bases using spikes should be left loose to reduce the chance of jamming a foot or ankle on a miscalculated slide. Hollywood-type bases, whose stems have broken off, are best saved and used for this purpose.

Third, all runners should be made to wear regulation helmets as they would during a game.

Finally, catchers must not be allowed to block the plate. Before the drills begin, this restriction must be explained.

These four considerations will help make the sliding aspects of these drills much safer without sacrificing the realism that sliding brings to the drills.

EPILOGUE

The old saying goes, "No one said it was going to be easy!" Unfortunately, when it comes to playing the outfield, players have never been told this. Instead, they have been made to believe that outfielding is the simplest to play of all the positions and, therefore, sits at the bottom of the ladder when it comes to talent requirements. As a consequence, the position has always carried with it a stigma and inferiority complex for those who have played it. It is no wonder, then, that the position is both played and coached from that point of view. Players and coaches too often think of outfielding as the least challenging and least complex of positions. This kind of thinking has gone on too long.

I hope these past many pages have opened or perhaps reopened the eyes of all to the position's many required talents, techniques, and strategies. As stated in the first chapter, some of these skills can hardly be taught. Instead, they must be natural...indeed, God-given! And while many of the related techniques and skills may be termed "coachable," players and coaches have discovered that often it is only through the grace of God that such skills can be mastered. Maybe the inferiority complex cast upon this position and those who play it has been lifted to some degree through the efforts that have gone into this book. Hopefully, the pride that belongs with the position of outfielding is back. If this book has helped to achieve that objective, then I have succeeded in mine. As a player or coach, then, may you, indeed, become outstanding in your field...the outfield, of course!